THE
AN ASSOCIATED PRESS
GUIDE TO GOOD NEWS WRITING

**RENE J.
CAPPON**

WORD

D0958446

Published by:
THE ASSOCIATED PRESS
50 Rockefeller Plaza
New York, N.Y. 10020

Library of Congress Catalog Card Number: 81-71142
ISBN: 0-917360-04-4
First Printing, October 1982   Second Printing, February 1983

To the often anonymous heroes of
The Associated Press, the editors, the
uncelebrated deskmen past and present
whose demands for accuracy, clarity
and taste have made the AP report a
standard for journalists, this book is
gratefully dedicated.

Keith Fuller
President and General Manager
The Associated Press

Contents

Wasted Words; Wasted Space ... The Anemia of Abstractions ... Up With People ... Muddling Modifiers ... Qualifiers: Hedge If You Must ... Put Verbs to Work ... Be Short, Familiar, Specific ... The Elegant Variation ... The Case for the Period ... Who's Who? ... Corral Those Participles ... Avoid Palling Passives ... Mismanaged Background

Don't Bury the News ... Try Writing "Visually" ... What's the Difference? ... Beware Overloads ... Horse First, Then Cart ... Control Yourself ... A Matter of Tension ... Action Speaks Louder ... Pitfalls of Attribution ... Second-Cycle Woes ... Watch the Bouncing Ball ... Legalistic Leads ... The Time Element

Foreword

This book is aimed at a select audience: those who care about precise and attractive use of the language.

If you are in that company, read on. For here you will find — in a mix of humor, common sense and only occasional editorial pique — a guide to help you achieve what should be every journalist's aim, telling the reader what you mean in a crisp and correct way.

Perhaps the problem is the speed with which daily journalists must do some of their work. Perhaps it is that sameness of some of what we write — today's baseball game being normally not very different from yesterday's, this week's council meeting straying into predictable clichés, today's newsbriefing advancing us little if at all toward better understanding of the subject.

Whatever the reasons, the problems that persist in everyday news writing are not hard to identify and it is to these that this manual speaks.

We talk here not of an idyllic newsroom where the final four-paragraph accounts of auto accidents can be the leisurely product of a third and fourth rewrite. No, we deal here with what the careful writer (and editor) can do in a busy newsroom to bring news copy the clarity and the appeal it must have at a time when so many other activities beckon for the reader's attention.

So good writing is a practical matter; the story must be well written if it is to be well read.

But, more tellingly, it is a professional matter. We should feel pride in doing our jobs well and in fulfilling our obligation to serve the reader well.

In the tumult of the last decade, as journalists have found themselves caught in unaccustomed legal and professional controversy, thousands of speeches have been given in defense of what we call "the people's right to know."

Let us also recognize the people's right to understand and be entertained. In support of these comes this guide for the careful use of our most precious asset — the word.

Louis D. Boccardi
Executive Editor and Vice President
The Associated Press

About the Author

From a writer's point of view, the best circumstance is to have Jack Cappon, in the flesh, as your editor. Next best is to have at hand, for consultation or merely occasional picnicking, a collection of his ideas on the use of the language.

This book provides such a larder. What it does not provide are the gurgles and the sighs and the groans that rise from behind his desk when he comes upon sentences that are particularly well turned or upon writing that is lazy or pompous or dull. What makes Jack Cappon an editor, and not just a blue penciller with an academic interest in syntax, is that his romance with the English language is visceral. When people who should know better abuse the language, Jack Cappon hurts.

You will catch the flavor of Cappon in the flesh as you meander through Cappon in print. In his chapter on quotes, for example, he refers to stock bromides that "have the appeal of bovine cud." In his discussion of overloaded leads, he cites an especially turgid one about a ballet performer and remarks, "It's a wonder the writer neglected to add the first nine bars from *Swan Lake*.." Vintage Cappon. Those are the sort of comments AP writers routinely find scribbled in the margins when he sends back their copy for reworking.

The name on his birth certificate, issued in Vienna in 1924, is René Jacques Cappon. (One preachment of this book is to prefer the plain word to the fancy one; "Jack" will do.) He grew up speaking German, which he still does, and Hungarian, which he has forgotten. English he started at school in Vienna, along with Latin and Greek, which he pursued in high school in New York but reluctantly dropped at the University of Iowa.

Of all those languages, English was the one that seduced him. In conversation with habitués of the AP Newsfeatures department, the "Poets' Corner" over which Cappon presides, he often muses aloud about the mystery of the language, the magic that makes certain combinations of words fit together, like notes in a musical score, while the same words in other combinations jar. He never tires of discussions of this sort.

Cappon is serving his second stint as AP Newsfeatures editor.

He held the job once before, from 1958 to 1962, after toiling in AP bureaus in Baltimore, Frankfurt and Kansas City. Later he became AP Managing Editor. As General News Editor, he again took over stewardship of the Poets' Corner in 1977.

Jack asked me to serve as editor of this book. The pleasure was mine, though the role reversal a bit strange. (Who will oversee the overseers?) He has chosen to cite as examples in his text a sentence or two of my origin. The eye and the ear and that chimerical thing in Jack Cappon called taste have improved the writer of those lines. Over the years, he has enhanced us all.

Jules Loh
Special Correspondent
The Associated Press

Author's Note

Any word book like *The Word* is, in a sense, a collaboration. My collaborators have been numerous; I count among them the people on the staffs of The Associated Press and AP member newspapers who have been subjected to writing workshops I have given over the past six or seven years.

Rather than a systematic journalism manual, the book is extended shoptalk — a continuation of the discussions, formal and informal, with newswriters intent on improving themselves in their craft.

Much news writing is, of course, done under deadline pressure, and it isn't always possible to hone and polish. But, too often, time limitations are invoked as an excuse for the kind of carelessness that springs more from poor writing habits than any other cause. Writers who trouble themselves about technique can adjust to these rush hours without turning slipshod.

Certain questions kept recurring at the workshops: How do I enliven my style? What's true color? How do I avoid limp leads without teetering into hysterical ones? What makes for good feature writing?

Much of *The Word* is devoted to such practical matters. I have tried to show what works, what doesn't, and why, as much by examples from copy as by commentary. These snippets of instructive prose stem mostly from the AP report, which was naturally handiest for me, with others from newspapers around the country.

I owe a debt to these largely anonymous contributors, triumphant or limping in the heat of the daily battle.

I also owe specific debts. I am especially grateful to AP Special Correspondent Jules Loh, who edited *The Word* with gentle wisdom. I owe thanks, too, to Executive Editor Lou Boccardi, who read the manuscript and offered valuable suggestions and criticism.

For errors that have slipped through this fine screening, I bear sole responsibility. I suppose that some will be found; a corollary to Murphy's Law states that anyone who writes a book on writing will inevitably commit some of the gaffes he warns against.

Some readers no doubt will find certain judgments of mine open to question — as too dogmatic, too lenient, or altogether wrongheaded. Perhaps so. What matters more to me is the hope that this work might stir some writers, new and old, to think more about the process of writing, to remember that the first duty of language is to communicate, and that words can be the best of friends or the worst of enemies.

R. J. C.
New York, 1982

The Word

LANGUAGE: Pompous, Pedantic and Plain

1

To say things clearly and concisely takes skill and, above all, vigilance. Bloated language is all around us. Government pumps gaseous bureaucratese into the environment. Other institutions, corporate headquarters, the professions and the social sciences diligently contribute to the effusion of jargon.

Reporters are professionally exposed to this strangling diction. Their job is to convert it into plain English. Unfortunately, many come down with a bad case of verbiage themselves, and then precision, clarity and grace desert them.

That's when we read of a man who *resigned his position to replenish his financial resources,* of the Air Force struggling to *minimize the aircraft's engine capability problems* and of *demands by the medical community to share in the government's decision-making process on health issues.*

In the reporters' better moments, they might have written, *who quit to earn more money, fix the plane's engine,* and *doctors' demands to have a say in government decisions on medical matters.*

The widespread tendency, especially among official "communicators," to clothe simple ideas in grandiose, obscure or evasive language has alarmed non-official word-watchers who believe language ought to mean something. One of them, NBC's Edwin Newman, subtitled *Strictly Speaking,* a witty diatribe on the subject, *Will America Be the Death of English?*

Probably not. But even non-fatal spasms of paralysis should not be taken lightly. Journalists have a special stake in this. Words are their tools. They cannot afford to turn them into fatty tissue.

Yet often they let themselves get stuck in the viscous verbiage of their sources. Even in the reporting on schools, a subject close to legions of readers, the pedagogue's jargon oozes into print. Libraries are elevated into resource centers. Classrooms become classroom situations, and classes become learning experiences. Kids who won't study for a learning experience are underachievers. The teacher's effort to encourage them becomes an effort to raise motivational levels. The principal who wants calm in the classroom proposes new goals in behavior modification. Little Marsha's shyness is difficulty to relate to her peer group.

None of this does much for the writer, and does much less for Mrs. Jones, the reader trying to learn what's going on in her local school.

The fatal lure of wordiness, abstraction and jargon is not new. Forty years ago George Orwell, master of the plain, forceful style, deplored the same tendencies.

Modern writing at its worst, he noted in his essay on "Politics and the English Language," doesn't choose words for the sake of their meaning but consists of "gumming long strips of words together that have already been set in order by someone else." He translated a verse from Ecclesiastes to illustrate the kind of prose this leads to:

I returned and saw under the sun, that the race is not to the swift, nor the battle to the strong, neither yet bread to the wise, nor yet riches to men of understanding, nor yet favor to men of skill; but time and chance happeneth to them all.

In modern English:

Objective consideration of contemporary phenomena compel the conclusion that success or failure in competitive activities exhibits no tendency to be commensurate with innate capacity, but that a considerable element of the unpredictable must invariably be taken into account.

This is parody, but not greatly overdrawn. Consider the following example. It purports to be an explanation of American foreign policy given a reporter by an unnamed State Department official. He need not have feared attribution; unlike Orwell's parody, it is entirely untranslatable:

What we are seeking to do is to forge an integrated political, economic and security mosaic that is structured to be responsive to local sensitivities while above all serving United States global interests and objectives, and in that sense this Pacific region is integrated conceptually with all we are doing in other regions.

Newswriters, of course, have their variant of jargon known as journalese. This plunges you into a hectic world where spectacles are colorful, fires are spectacular and sweep but never burn, where rivers rampage and explosions rip, while tornadoes leave their trail of death and destruction for grim-faced rescue workers while heavily armed (though usually club-wielding) police fend off potential looters; where massive demonstrations fuel angry confrontations, where dissenters always stalk, never walk, from the hall as the speaker blasts, raps, lambastes or lashes out at the foes who have vowed to defeat him; where investigations are always massive and murders brutal, to distinguish them from the gentle murders, where anything a reporter didn't expect is a surprise move and a metropolis is rocked by a city hall scandal that actually leaves nine-tenths of the population yawning.

The trouble with this kind of writing is not that it's unclear, but that it is tired. It tries to create artificial excitement and produces the opposite effect. It makes for stock melodrama that has long gone stale.

"Clear your mind of cant," Dr. Johnson once exhorted his biographer, Boswell. The message is similar to Orwell's, and is sound advice for newswriters as well. Clear your mind of the cant of officialese, the prefabricated phrase and hand-me-down wordings, and you'll begin to move from the swamplands of language to the bracing highlands. Here's a passage from a story by AP's Hal Boyle, whose mind habitually operated in those upper reaches:

> OMAHA BEACH, Normandy (AP) — It is D-Day plus five years, soldier, on this sandy coast where the world hinged on what you did.
>
> Because you did well here your world at home is as good as it is and if it isn't any better, why they'll have to blame someone else. There are some things you can do with a gun and there are other things you can't.
>
> What's it like here now, soldier, five years after you landed and put the first torch to Adolf Hitler's Western Wall?
>
> Well, the best answer might come from Pvt. Anthony R. Calif, or his neighbor, Pfc. Marvin C. Garness, or his neighbor, Lt. George W. Phillips, who has become a buddy of Staff Sgt. Miles S. Lewis.
>
> They have all settled here together, and they are all quiet men.
>
> But they wouldn't be interested so much in telling you what it's like now.
>
> They'd rather ask you: "What's it like now at home? And my folks — are they well and happy?"
>
> For they came here to stay, silent citizens of a silent American city on foreign soil. They rest with 9,523 other soldiers in the U.S. military cemetery atop a high green hill overlooking Omaha Beach.

This is straightforward and effective. No prefabricated phrases are stripped into the passage — *supreme sacrifice, made the world a better place in which to live, did not die in vain,* etc. Boyle used only seven modifiers and no fancy words; strikingly, only 32 of the 183 words (not counting the names) are longer than one syllable.

Not every news subject can be handled in exactly that style, but all news writing should aim at that sort of simplicity and directness, equally removed from noisy journalese or stodgy abstraction. That is the message of this book. All the rest is amplification.

NEWS WRITING: Information Is Not Enough

2

Writing is the art of the second thought. What first springs to mind is seldom good enough; the skill lies not in a ready gush of words, but in sifting them. Sometimes that process is swift, sometimes it takes longer, but second thought there must be even — or especially — under the time pressures of daily journalism.

By good enough I mean copy that's clear, precise, succinct and expressive. To be informative is not enough; the information must be presented in ways that strike home, with a direct bearing on the reader.

Clarity, precision and the rest are genial qualities of the plain style. They overlap and reinforce one another, but they rarely attend us unbidden. They must be coaxed and cultivated.

Writers should ask themselves at least three questions before letting go of a story:

1. Have I said what I meant to say? This writer mistakenly thought so:

BETHLEHEM, Pa. — Job prospects for some college graduates
— especially those with engineering degrees and women — improved
for the second successive year, the College Placement Center says.

2. Have I put it as concisely as possible? The writer of the
following sentence, from a story about a California brush
fire, may well have thought so:

Twelve rescue ambulances stood by to rush injured persons to
nearby hospitals.

But on second thought it becomes clear that eight of
those 12 words are drones. Ambulances are rescue vehicles;
they don't dawdle; they always carry the injured, not the
hale and hearty; and they rarely search for the remoter hospitals. Four words were all that were needed: *Twelve ambulances stood by*.

3. Have I put things as simply as possible?

The relationship between Congress and bureaucrats is one of
symbiosis.

Now of course you know what symbiosis means. The
word, from biology, fits the sense, and this case may be ar-
guable. But is the word, opaque to many readers, really necessary? *Congress and bureaucrats feed on each other* expresses the same idea in language everybody can understand.

Details, you might say. But attention to detail is at the
heart of good writing. As many a sports announcer would
comment, it's a game of inches. Get careless with clauses
and a sentence turns into a black hole from which no light
escapes. Misplace a modifier and a serious passage becomes
a grinning farce. Let an indefinite pronoun float free of its
moorings, and you create a mystery about who does what
to whom.

There's no solace in the thought that many readers will

be able to figure out a muddled sentence. They should not be asked to. They should not be required to guess, to pause, to backtrack, or slog through a swamp of superfluous words.

Nowhere is the case for economy with words stated more persuasively than in *The Elements of Style* by William Strunk and E. B. White:

> Vigorous writing is concise. A sentence should contain no unnecessary words, a paragraph no unnecessary sentences, for the same reason that a drawing should contain no unnecessary lines and a machine no unnecessary parts. This requires not that a writer make all his sentences short, or that he avoid all detail and treat his subject only in outline, but that every word tell.

Wasted Words, Wasted Space

Hardly a newswriter in honorable practice today is not aware, in theory, of the need to save readers time and newspapers space, and no principle is so widely ignored in practice.

It's a matter of habit, starting with the small, innocuous phrase: *in the event of* for *if, despite the fact that* for *in spite of, adverse weather conditions* for *bad weather, impact negatively on* for *hurt* or *damage.*

Many sentences can be improved by surface trimming. In the following example, just omit the italicized words:

> WASHINGTON — The Reagan administration is writing *new* regulations *designed* to sweep away many years of *accumulated* red tape and let local governments decide *for themselves* how to spend major urban aid grants.

Often, slight rewording produces dramatic results. Compare the original sentence (left) with the revision on the right:

It is unusual in the Legislature to have a conference committee of more than four members.

A conference committee with more than four members is unusual.

The IRS said that a number of Oregon complaints had been received as of Friday. Investigators are now in the process of checking out the possible violations.

The IRS said a number of Oregon complaints had been received as of Friday. Investigators are checking them.

Consumers were slower in repaying installment debt in August and quicker in adding new debt in August than earlier this year, the government reported.

Consumers were quicker to borrow and slower to repay in August than earlier this year, the government reported.

Six, seven and six words are saved, respectively. The aim is not simply to save words, but to improve writing. The shorter versions are invariably crisper. Look how eliminating dullness and saving words go hand in hand in these examples:

Peking *is not in favor of* arms sales to Taiwan.

. . . opposes . . .

The Senate Ethics Committee can vote *for the expulsion of* . . .

. . . to expel . . .

The union will *conduct a* poll of its members.

. . . poll . . .

The Iranians hope *for the re-equipment of* their armed forces.

. . . to re-equip . . .

Repetition, the grossest form of wordiness, results from poor organization. The danger is greatest in the use of quotes:

MIAMI — Faced with a summer travel slump, Eastern Airlines ignited a fare war Monday as it reintroduced discount coupons, dropping the lowest one-way fare price from New York to California to $134.

Two of Eastern's chief competitors, American Airlines and Pan American World Airways, immediately said they would match the new fares.

"We have and always will remain competitive," said Pan Am spokesman Harvey Berman in New York. "Anything we can do to remain competitive we will do."

American Airlines spokesman Al Becker added: "It's fair to say that we will be there with a program of our own. We simply must and will be competitive.

Each spokesman is allowed to say twice what's already conveyed in the preceding paragraph.

Every day's news copy throws up a flock of short phrases which, on second thought, prove grossly inflated. Here's a typical sampling of what writers said and what, in the context, they meant:

announced the names of	identified
Detroit area residential and real estate holdings	houses in the Detroit area
responds specifically to incidents	responds to incidents
for the entire distance of the flight	for the flight
use his persuasive powers on behalf of	support
not yet known	unknown
can produce liver degeneration	can damage livers

so it can afford to re-equip its fleet with new, fuel-efficient jets	so it can buy fuel-efficient jets
now is asking for the relaxation of	wants to relax

The Anemia of Abstractions

Certain abstract nouns, perennials of newspaper usage, tend to create clusters of surplus words: *issue, case, situation, question, condition, facilities, activities, experience, field, factor, proposition, basis, character, nature, process, problem*. Often these nouns are tacked on to specific words, as when *heavy traffic* becomes *heavy traffic problem* or *congested traffic situation*.

In addition to a certain stuffiness, these nouns are vague and abstract. What is a facility, an issue, a problem? A facility can be an airport, a hotel, a park or a kitchen. An issue is anything people discuss or disagree about. A health problem can be anything from an ingrown toenail to terminal cancer.

A man who gets his throat slit in a dark alley is *a victim of violence,* but much is lost in the transcription. That is how abstract words work. Call a spade a spade and you evoke a precise picture. Call it an agricultural implement and you might be talking about a plow, a rake, or an air-conditioned tractor.

Obviously these long-faced, abstract nouns have their places, but the following examples show why you should treat them with reserve:

The *situation* poses a danger to the public because of the tendency of persons on probation to commit more crimes.	It's risky because people on probation often commit crimes.

On the *issue* of welfare payments, the committee deferred action for three weeks.

The committee deferred action on welfare payments for three weeks.

The government decided to replace him with a general of more aggressive *character*.

. . . replace him with a more aggressive general.

Crimes of a violent *nature* are increasing.

Violent crimes are increasing.

The Legislature has threatened to suspend all strip mining *operations*.

. . . all strip mining.

Ample space for recreational *activities* was provided.

Ample space for recreation was provided.

The bridge below Smithville has now become a practical *proposition*.

. . . has become feasible.

The loss of skilled workers will be a crippling *factor* in the economy of Iran.

. . . will cripple the economy of Iran.

Another worrisome matter is the *question* of productivity.

Another worry is productivity.

They receive their checks on a monthly *basis*.

They receive monthly checks.

They agreed that their adventure in the woods had been a worthwhile *experience*.

. . .had been worthwhile.

Mathematics skills are considered a valuable learning *experience*.

They can learn much from mathematics.

He is an acknowledged leader in the medical *field*.

He is a leader in medicine.

Half of the town lives in *conditions* of abject poverty.

. . . lives in abject poverty.

The state's hospital *facilities* must be upgraded.	The state's hospitals must be upgraded.
A doubling of the patrol was suggested as a solution to the *problem* of crime.	Doubling the patrol was suggested to deal with crime.

The prepositional phrase *in terms of* enjoys a peculiar vogue today, perhaps because of its technical aura. Useful in expressing specific relationships — *The dollar is worth less in terms of the Japanese yen* — it is frequently misused in ways that turn sentences into fudge:

In terms of home prices and availability, young couples today are virtually excluded from the housing market.	Few young couples today can find houses they can afford.
The company pledged improvements *in terms of* labor relations and efficiency.	The company pledged to improve labor relations and efficiency.

Up With People

Under the heading of "abstractitis," Fowler's *Dictionary of Modern English Usage* notes: "Persons and what they do, things and what is done to them, are put in the background, and we can only peer at them as through a glass, darkly."

Here's an example:

Research has shown that accidents are proportionately more prevalent with motorcycle use and are of a more violent nature.

Nothing in that sentence acts on anything. There's no hint that it has anything to do with people. The following revision puts it more concretely:

Research has shown that motorcyclists have more accidents proportionately than other motorists, and are more often killed or seriously injured.

Another instance:

It is difficult to measure or quantify the impact of the energy crisis in terms of plant closings and job losses.	It's hard to say how many workers have lost their jobs and how many plants have closed because of the energy shortage.

The revised version puts human beings into the act, gets rid of *impact, crisis, in terms of* and the redundant *measure* and *quantify,* and converts two abstract nouns — *losses* and *closings* — into active verbs. There's a difference.

Contrast the next two passages with the revisions:

A state civil service examination to fill uniformed court officers jobs "had grossly disproportionate impact on blacks and Hispanics as compared to whites," it was charged in a federal court suit today.	A state civil service examination to fill jobs for uniformed court officers was unfair to blacks and Hispanics, a federal court suit charged today.

Was unfair to expresses specifically what takes 13 words of jargon in the original. Note also how the unpleasant noun pileup, *uniformed court officers jobs,* was loosened with a preposition.

Utilities were under mandate Wednesday not to cut off service during the winter months to *individuals whose health might thus be endangered.*	Utilities were under orders Wednesday not to cut off service to the elderly and seriously ill.

The dead hand of abstraction weighs on the last part of the original lead.

Here are needless abstract blotches in an action story:

Police are "furious" over a *recent rash of objects* being thrown from highway overpasses at moving vehicles and say they are going to crack down on the *offenders* "before someone gets killed."

Police Detective John Smith said police have not been able to link recent wrecks involving serious injuries with the *overpass offenses* but added: "We just think that some recent accidents are related to this. It just seems too much of a coincidence."

As the story notes later, the youths were tossing bottles, rocks and bricks, which is livelier than *recent rash of objects.* Let details drive out generalities:

> Police, furious at youngsters who toss rocks, bricks and bottles from overpasses at moving cars, intend to crack down "before someone gets killed."
> Detective John Smith said no highway smashup has been linked to the rock-throwers but added . . .

Be careful in writing crime and accident stories, though. For all that has been said, it is possible to be too specific, especially with gory details. When a body long dead is recovered, it's superfluous to mention that it was *badly decomposed.* Nor was it useful to report, in a plane crash story, that *the flesh fell off some of the victims* who burned to death. *Charred beyond recognition* is another phrase you can usually dispense with. A man stabbed 20 times may be presumed to have bled; the writer need not dwell on the dimensions of a *pool of blood.* Limit the gore. For that matter, you often find a crime victim described as *fully clothed,* a gratuitous particular when there is no reason to suspect otherwise.

You can't avoid abstract words entirely. They save space. But precede them with particulars; if you write of facilities, let the reader first be clear on what these facilities are. In stories that deal in abstractions, give concrete examples: The *tight housing market* is also an old lady evicted with her four cats.

The following story is from the diplomatic beat. The reader is hard pressed to glean a clear fact from the first four paragraphs:

> WASHINGTON — Less than two weeks before President Carter's meeting with President José López Portillo of Mexico, there is little

prospect for a solution of *nagging problems* that have troubled *relations* between the two countries for several years.

So, while officials acknowledge they would have liked to stage an impressive treaty-signing ceremony, they are now billing the meetings as a *working session* that will *produce few tangible results.*

Under Carter and López Portillo, the United States and Mexico have at least talked regularly to each other, even though they have *not agreed on many issues.* The two agreed in 1977 to set up a *"consultative mechanism,"* which means that diplomats from both sides meet regularly on *specific issues.*

Administration officials say the sessions have provided a form for *exchanging viewpoints,* and may yet lead to an agreement on *tough issues on the agenda.*

This dustup of Foggy Bottom lingo tells you little more than that the president will meet to discuss *problems* and *issues.* What are they? What's dividing the two countries? True, the story now begins to mention particulars, quarrels over oil prices, crop imports, illegal immigrants, but by this time the reader's eyes have glazed over.

The story would have started more auspiciously with particulars:

> WASHINGTON — Less than two weeks before President Carter's meeting with President Jóse López Portillo of Mexico, chances look slim for settling disputes over illegal immigration, tomato imports and oil prices.
>
> These and other matters have bedeviled relations between the two countries for years . . .

Muddling Modifiers

Not every noun needs an adjective. Not every adjective needs an adverb. Not every writer has gotten the message.

E. B. White, who knows about clear prose, notes that the adjective hasn't been born yet that can pull a noun out of a tight spot. Mark Twain, who also had writing experience, once told a young correspondent, "When you can catch an adjective, kill it."

He softened that a little: "No, I don't mean that utterly, but kill the most of them — then the rest will be valuable. They weaken when they are close together, they give strength when wide apart. An adjective habit, or a wordy, flowery, diffuse habit, once fastened upon a person is as hard to get rid of as any other vice."

Some writers equate adjective-killing with clubbing baby seals, but strong writing rests on nouns and verbs. Pick the right ones and you'll need few modifiers. They should be used to make your meaning clear, not as decorative afterthoughts.

It is hard to see what the second adjective is doing in this sentence:

> The shots on the quiet Sunday morning sent passersby into *frightened* flight.

Quiet, yes. But *frightened flight?* To distinguish it from courageous flight?

The lust for modification leads writers into many other futilities. Certain nouns evoke inevitable adjectives that are only feebly descriptive. The combinations become clichés: *Posh* resort, *sprawling* reservation, *hardy* natives, *devout* Catholic, *scenic* countryside, *colorful* scene, *high-powered* rifle, and many more.

An onslaught of modifiers turns the following story into treacle:

> LONDON — The *slim, almost boyish* figure of the next king of England moved across the *thick* carpet of the *elegant* Brown's Hotel at Piccadilly. He signed the hotel register as cameras flashed.
>
> En route back to the *enormous, black* Rolls Royce outside, he suddenly stopped. He had spotted two young women working on a guest register in the lobby.
>
> "What are you doing?" he inquired *politely* in *deep aristocratic* tones.
>
> The receptionists looked up and their jaws fell.
>
> "The guest register, is it?" asked the *immaculately groomed* Prince Charles.

You would expect a prince to be polite and immaculately groomed and to visit an elegant hotel rather than a fleabag. Anyway, *thick carpet* suggests elegance. And what is *almost boyish?* What are *deep aristocratic tones?* Strike all modifiers except *thick, enormous, black* and *slim,* and the intro recovers.

Keep your hands off nouns that need no additional voltage. *Serious* danger, *stern* warning, *deadly* poison, *grave* crisis are examples; the nouns do better without the modifiers.

A crisis is, of course, a serious turning point by definition. But the habit of automatic-modifying leads to many other redundancies, among them:

absolutely conclusive	lonely hermit
agricultural crops	meaningless gibberish
awkward dilemma	mutual cooperation
close proximity	new record
complete monopoly	old adage
completely full	organic life
divisive quarrel	original founder
end result	patently obvious
entirely absent	personal friend
exact counterpart	personal opinion
future plan	present incumbent
general public	true facts
grateful thanks	ultimate outcome
hired mercenary	violent explosion
irreducible minimum	vitally necessary

To test the logic of such knee-jerk modifiers, turn them around. Are there gentle explosions? Pleasant dilemmas? False facts? Impersonal friends?

Treat adverbial intensifiers with the same reserve as adjectives. *Very urgent, highly unusual, extremely serious* — the adverbs add only shrillness.

Definitely is generally expendable. *The ambassador will*

definitely leave tomorrow says nothing more than that he'll leave. *Undue* can be particularly fatuous:

The government cautioned against *undue* alarm over Skylab.

They didn't mean that there was reason for due alarm. They meant there was no cause for alarm.

The conservative group complained that the court was taking *undue* liberties with the Constitution.

Strike *undue*. Adverbs like *relatively* and *comparatively* are usually mere padding:

Relatively few senators answered the quorum call.

The number of football injuries is *comparatively* high this year.

Relative or compared with what?

Qualifiers: Hedge If You Must

Qualifiers are necessary in statements open to doubt. Because news reports are often based on partial information, some hedging is inevitable: *Possibly, perhaps, probably, reportedly, on the whole,* and so on.

Some writers are so habituated — or so insecure — that they guard their flanks with qualifiers even when the flank needs no guarding.

Dingell, it can *probably* be said with *absolute certainty* . . .

Either *probably* or *absolute certainty* but not both.

WILMINGTON, Del. — A man who *allegedly* hijacked a Piedmont Airlines prop jet *reportedly* was subdued by passengers while the plane was in flight and taken into custody when the plane landed here, authorities said.

Sheriff's deputies said one or more passengers jumped the man while the plane was flying over Wilmington . . .

Unless the writer thought the authorities and sheriff's

deputies were hallucinating, there was no need for the qualifiers.

Here's a case of a modifier, itself unnecessary, qualified into never-never land:

> Saudi Arabia's *almost* single-minded obsession with Israel . . .

An obsession implies single-mindedness. You're either single-minded or you aren't. If the writer suspected his assertion, he should have made the noun *preoccupation* and scuttled the adjective and adverb.

Look hard at *basically, essentially, fundamentally* & Co., which are usually superfluous.

> *Basically,* the company plans to emphasize retailing.

You're not obligated to give every aspect of the company's plan. If what you left out is important, put it in. If not, forget the qualifier.

> They are called something else here, but *essentially* they work as security guards.

If that's what they do essentially, good enough:

> While they are called something else, they work as security guards.

> *In simplest terms,* the theory holds that . . .

That implies condescension to readers who can't be expected to grasp it otherwise. You're supposed to be writing in simplest terms, and there's no need to advertise.

Put Verbs to Work

The verb, particularly in the active voice, is ringmaster of the sentence. It sets pace and movement. A peculiarity of abstract writing is an aversion to strong verbs, which are thinned out into combinations of weak verb, abstract noun and modifier.

The refugees starved in their mountain retreat becomes *the refugees experienced severe hunger in their mountain retreat. The economy rebounded* slows into *the economy showed a sudden, sharp improvement.*

Other symptoms of noun plague:

determined the truth of	verified
established conclusive evidence of	proved
held a meeting	met
prove of benefit to	benefited
put in an appearance	appeared
reached an agreement	agreed
submitted his resignation	resigned
take into consideration	consider
take into custody	arrest, seize

Occasionally the wordier form is justified to capture a nuance. *Reach an agreement* suggests a longer effort, perhaps, than *agree.* Usually, however, the single verb will do.

Effect and *impact* are devourers of more precise verbs:

Teachers as well as parents have much *impact* on students' career choices	. . . influence students' career choices.
The boycott had no *effect* on sales.	. . . did not reduce sales.
The prosecutor's statement had an obvious *effect* on the jury.	. . . swayed the jury.

Be Short, Familiar, Specific

From what we have seen about the combat against clutter, vagueness and officialese, certain precepts come into focus. They are not new. They were derived long ago from the practice of good writers. Consider them a potent charm against the legion of devils that try to turn prose into fudge:

Prefer the short word to the long.
Prefer the familiar word to the fancy.
Prefer the specific word to the abstract.
Use no more words than necessary to make your meaning clear.

None of this means that long or unfamiliar words should never be used. Sometimes they fit the meaning best. Occasionally they serve the rhythm of a sentence. But there must be good reasons for the choice. It's hard to see any advantage to long words such as those in the left-hand column:

accommodations	rooms
ameliorate	improve
approximately	about
commence	begin
deactivate	close, shut off
endeavor	try
finalize	end, complete
implement	carry out
in consequence of	because
initiate	begin
methodology	method
objective	aim, goal
prior to	before
proliferation	spread
purchase	buy
remuneration	pay
replicate	repeat
socialize	mingle, meet, make friends
substantial proportion	many, much
underprivileged	poor
utilize	use

The Elegant Variation

Writers reach for big words because they consider them more elegant. The same mistaken impulse drives them into the "elegant variation." This is done under the pretext of avoiding repetition, but there are better ways to do that than by fancy synonyms that often don't fit well:

> The mayor's task force was asked to meet with the owners of the *structures,* discuss whether they wanted their *buildings* preserved, and recommend ways to adapt older *edifices* to new uses.

This grates, and in any case *edifices* means something more grandiose than intended. If the writer didn't want to use *buildings* three times in the sentence, a pronoun should have been called to the rescue:

> . . . to meet with the owners of the buildings, discuss whether they wanted *them* preserved, and recommend ways to adapt the older ones to new uses.

The Case for the Period

Sentences come under special pressures in news writing. A lot of facts need to be marshaled concisely, usually in the order of decreasing news value (the "inverted pyramid") with background details to be worked in. Writers are often tempted to overload. It's best to limit a sentence to one idea, or a range of closely related ones. Otherwise a sentence can march off in several directions at once:

> The former mental patient who took seven women hostage when police broke up his robbery of a jewelry store held two sisters early Tuesday after the other five escaped, including one woman he shot and wounded, police said.

The route to sanity is two sentences:

> A former mental patient, besieged by police in a jewelry store he had tried to rob, still held two sisters hostage early Tuesday. Five other women hostages managed to get away, though one of them was shot and wounded by the gunman as she fled, authorities said.

Relative clauses run riot in the following exhibit:

> "They might be more comfortable voting that way," explained Sylvia Frank, a member of the local school board and the planning

board in Steingut's 41st Assembly District, who was one of the organizers of the petition campaign to form the new party.

Steingut lost the Sept. 12 primary to Murray Weinstein, 50, an attorney, who was a last-minute substitute for his daughter, Helene, who was thrown off the ballot because she lived in Manhattan, outside the Assembly district.

Each sentence should be split into two.

Short sentences are more likely to be clear than long ones, and copy with a high proportion of short sentences is apt to be more readable. An *average* sentence length of 16 words seems about right. An average of 20 would be an outer limit (a few writers are uncommonly good at constructing longer sentences). You'll find that examples of good writing cited in this book (by Hal Boyle, Jules Loh, Walter Mears, Sid Moody and Saul Pett) collectively average out at 16 words per sentence. Note that this is the average, leaving plenty of leeway for longer sentences, and shorter ones, to avoid monotony.

A succession of short, loose sentences creates an unpleasant "See Spot run" sing-song:

The assailant forced Sabo out of the van and tied him up. He then forced Miss Sawicky to the rear of the van and threatened to rape her.

Sabo managed to get free and began fighting with the man. As they struggled, Miss Sawicky ran to a nearby apartment building owned by her father.

Her father ran to the scene, and he and Sabo fought with the assailant, police said. Sabo and Sawicky were hit by several shots.

In every sentence, long or short, take care that related words don't drift apart. The modifier should be close to the words it modifies, the verb to its subject.

A videotape camera installed in a San Diego market filmed the fatal stabbing outside the store of a 31-year-old woman, authorities say.

Was the woman killed or did she own the store? Make it:

. . . *filmed the fatal stabbing of a 31-year-old woman outside the store.*

The following three examples also need to be reworded:

A disc jockey who climbed Mount Rainier for charity and his two guides got a lift from the weather . . .

Police said both men had lived in Newark and are considered dangerous.

A Harlem man who disappeared a month ago was found slain by his wife in the trunk of the couple's car, police said.

Who's Who?

Pronoun pain ensues from placement that leaves the antecedent in doubt:

He said he is certain it's an original de Torres painting, worth $200,000. The artist's signature is on it and *it* includes the faces of his favorite models, he said.

The pronoun refers to *painting,* not the signature, which would have been worth $200,000 by itself with all those faces in it. Also, at first glance *he said* seems to refer to the dead artist, not the curator who was speaking.

For most of the debate, Carter kept his challenger on the defensive — explaining that *his* views on arms control, military programs and social security were not the "very dangerous" and even "radical" notions that the president said they were.

Who is explaining whose views? It's the challenger defending his position, but you have to read the sentence several times to be sure.

Pronoun vagueness totally eclipses meaning in the following:

MINEHEAD, England — A man who claims politician Jeremy Thorpe had a homosexual affair with him and then plotted his death to conceal it testified Thursday *he* lied in some previous statements.

Thorpe denies the allegations of Norman Scott, 38, who made several angry outbursts as Thorpe's lawyer led *him* back over *his* statements to police that he said included "dreadful lies" about the way Thorpe approached him sexually in 1961.

Who lied? And did Thorpe's lawyer lead Thorpe or Scott over previous statements?

Corral Those Participles

Dangling participles are ancient blunders that keep claiming new victims:

> WASHINGTON — President Carter said Tuesday he does not believe the national anthem's stature is diminished by being played before sports events.

Federal law should prohibit playing with stature in public.

> A few hours earlier the salesman had made an appointment with Campbell, whom he had never met before.
> While eating dinner in the hotel restaurant later, a boyishlooking, pink-skinned man with premature gray hair and dressed in a blue jump suit bounded up to the table.

Interesting, but poor for the digestion.

Avoid Palling Passives

Use the active voice whenever possible. *Police arrested John Smith* is shorter and crisper than *John Smith was arrested by police.* Occasionally, of course, news value dictates a passive; if you were writing about *Mayor* John Smith, you'd want to lead with his name.

In most cases, though, the passive is flabby, dropping the doer of a deed out of the picture.* That's why officialese is addicted to the passive mode. *It is believed* or *it is esti-*

---

*— *The distinction between wishy-washy passive and firm active can be ominously practical. Psychology Today reported that a specialist in the analysis of extortion notes and terrorist threats considers, among other things, what form the writer uses. A note that says "I will kill you" suggests the sender means business. "You will be killed," on the other hand, suggests that the writer may waver, lacking "sufficient commitment to identify himself as the agency of the threat."*

mated allows the estimator and the believer to vanish in the fog.

The following example shows how much weaker the passive sentence can be than the active:

The announced rejection by demonstrators of West Germany's security policy had led to its being denounced by Chancellor Schmidt as "a declaration of war" on the government.	The demonstrators' rejection of West Germany's security policy led Chancellor Schmidt to denounce their stand as a "declaration of war" on the government.

The revision is clearer and more direct.

The verb *to be* offers little action. Sentences that start with a *there is* construction usually flow like molasses. In the following example, the rewrite, with its reliance on active verbs, invigorates the entire passage:

There was no police escort to clear the way. There were no flower cars or mourners. There was only a single gray hearse carrying Robert Moses across the monuments that he built.	No police escort cleared the way. No flower cars or limousines with mourners followed the gray hearse that carried Robert Moses across the monuments he built.
They said there would be no cortege. They were wrong. On every road and bridge that bore his name or imprint, there was an endless stream of cars and vans and trucks and buses.	They said there would be no cortege. They were wrong. Cars and vans and trucks and buses, an endless stream, rolled over every road and bridge that bore his name or imprint.

A sentence should be emphatic. When possible, express even a negative in positive form:

The Legislature did not consider the governor's proposal.	The Legislature ignored the governor's proposal.
The company said not all absentees had no excuse.	The company said some absentees had excuses.

Mismanaged Background

Badly placed background detail in a story often produces sentences with wildly disparate ideas. *Born in Detroit, he was an ardent stamp collector* is the kind of non sequitur one finds in many obituaries. The havoc caused by background material worked in without regard for logic and relevance is shown in the following passages from a second-day story on Elvis Presley's death. The writer struggled to tell essentials of the singer's career within the framework of developing news, and some of the sentences flop around like beached fish:

> Dr. George Nichopulos, longtime physician to the swivel-hipped, throaty baritone who was known as the King of Rock 'n' Roll, said an autopsy revealed a constriction in one of the arteries to the heart, which restricted blood flow and brought on a heart attack.
>
> Presley, whose recording of "Heartbreak Hotel" helped put him on top of the entertainment world 21 years ago, was discovered unconscious at Graceland in suburban Memphis Tuesday afternoon.
>
> The doctor said attempts to revive Presley, who appeared in 31 films — including "Love Me Tender" and "Jailhouse Rock" — continued because of a slight chance that life still existed in his body.

In the next example, too, the misplaced details interfere with the flow of thought. The story is about a man who survived a long fall when his parachute failed to open.

> The son of a postal worker, Mongillo was living in Florida when he had his brush with death.
>
> Mongillo, whose only income is $100 a month from a local welfare fund, said, "I was scared. I knew I was going to die."

The answer to such difficulties is to disengage and regroup. In the Presley story, the facts about his death, the resuscitation effort and the autopsy belong in one section of the story, the facts of his rise to fame, film credits and song hits in another. In the Mongillo story, a separate paragraph should have wrapped up his postal antecedents and poverty, leaving the flow of thought unimpaired.

Where background details can be interwoven smoothly with the news development or narrative, it's the preferred way. Where they chop up the story and the logic of individual sentences, it's best to present the material in a coherent paragraph or two at an appropriate place in the story.

Useful as the inverted pyramid is — and indispensable for fastbreaking stories — it harbors a risk. The sequence of central events is sometimes left foggy. Readers are told what happened, but not always how, in what order. Careful writers will sort it out in a clear, chronological summary somewhere in the story after they have disposed of the main news points. Often matters are left like this:

> Wielding homemade knives, the inmates commandeered a milk truck, which they used to vault over a 25-foot wall, he said. The group then threw Molotov cocktails made with paint thinner at a guard tower and leaped from the top of the truck.

When did they vault? When did they leap?

In the following example, a simple sequence becomes twisted by needless *befores* and *afters*:

Last Wednesday, the 3-year-old monkey escaped from a backyard leash and bit a woman and her son *after* jumping into their passing car.

Neighbor Debbie Jackson testified that, before the attack, the monkey was taunted by several youths who raced at it with bicycles and screamed.

After the biting, Columbo climbed into a tree and descended only *after* a boy coaxed him down with sliced bananas.

Last Wednesday, Columbo slipped his leash and escaped from Coleman's backyard.

A neighbor testiified that screaming youngsters raced at Columbo with their bicycles. The frightened monkey jumped into a passing car and bit the driver and her son.

Columbo then climbed into a tree and stayed there until a boy coaxed him down with banana slices.

Clean and lean sentences flourish best in a well-organized story. We have seen how mishandling of background gums up the machinery. That is largely a matter of organization. Jumping back and forth results in excess wordage and tires the reader. Complete each topic before going on to the next.

In structure and sentence: Simplify. Avoid clutter. Prune. Think twice.

LEADS:
The Agony of
Square One

3

There is no getting around it, although every writer sometimes wishes there were: Every story must have a beginning. A lead. Incubating a lead is a cause of great agony. Why is no mystery. Based on the lead, a reader makes a critical decision: Shall I go on?

Don't be intimidated by leads, however. Think of them as though they cost you 10 bucks per word, each word to be engraved on stainless steel while you're sitting on a hot stove. Think economy.

A good lead makes a clear statement of the essential news point and when possible includes a detail that distinguishes the story from others of its kind. If the bank robbers escaped *in a baby blue Mercedes,* that small fact belongs in the lead.

The lead should have maximum effect with minimum of phrase. It must not mumble. Mumblers come from a variety of causes:

- A gaggle of secondary detail
- Abstract and general language
- Vagueness

• Stress on how something is announced rather than what is said, or on how the news originates rather than the news itself

• Entanglement in the chronology of an event

Following is a mumbler *in extremis:*

> Some marijuana and heroin were seized, says Park County Sheriff Bob Stokes, and though it wasn't a big drug raid, "it was the biggest seizure people-wise I have ever seen."

That is one of the oddest sentences, lead-wise, I have ever seen. As a mumbler, it is a classic because it says nothing. You had to dig into the third and fourth grafs of the story to make the point informatively:

> A narcotics raid on a private home netted small quantities of marijuana and heroin, Sheriff Bob Stokes says, but an amazing number of people — 73.
> "I only expected 10 or 15," Stokes said.

Even a short, direct lead can be a mumbler:

> TULSA — An attempted robbery at the Mansfield State Bank was not carried out today.

This violates the principle that readers should be told what is rather than what isn't. *Failed* would have been a better verb, but the lead is simply too sparse to work.

Don't Bury the News

Next, a more representative mumbler. The news point is made, but half buried, and the phrasing is abstract and formal, like an entry in an official record:

> The St. Claire Hospital's board of trustees has voted unanimously not to appeal a New Jersey Supreme Court ruling that allows Karen Anne Quinlan's father to have her life-support system disconnected, a spokesman said today.

The reader must wallow through two-thirds of the sentence before the news becomes visible. Human fate is ver-

balized as *having her life-support system disconnected.*
The following rewrite goes to the heart of the matter:

> The New Jersey hospital where Karen Anne Quinlan has lain in a coma for nearly a year will not challenge a court decision granting her the right to "death with dignity."

Who voted what and how is secondary detail that can come later. The news point is the decision not to appeal and what that means. The "death with dignity" quote appeared later in the story; it should have been in the lead. Note, too, how much closer the second example is to conversational language. If you read both leads aloud, you'll find the first phrased in a way no human being ever talks. Writing is not transcribed conversation, but good writing is never that remote from spoken idiom.

Here's a lead that is all generalized background:

> The centuries-old battle over separation of church and state is coming up again in an unusual fight over efforts to unionize lay teachers in the Los Angeles Roman Catholic Archdiocese.

Spare us, O Lord, erudition. Give us action:

> The Roman Catholic Archdiocese of Los Angeles is contesting the government's right to hold a union election among lay teachers on grounds that it would breach the separation between church and state.
>
> Diocesan schools, the suit contends, are part of the church and therefore off limits to government intervention.

Here's a lead that starts out strongly enough but stumbles to a mumble at the end:

> The City Council has passed a law banning families with children aged 14 or under from certain parts of town.

Certain parts? Care to say which? Near the old swimming hole perhaps? Well, residential communities for senior citizens. That's what the lead should have specified, along with other material found down in the story:

> Landlords in senior citizens' communities who sell or rent to families with young children face jail terms and fines under an ordinance passed by the City Council.

Here is a terminal mumbler. Only one word has a semblance of news interest, and it is hard to spot amid the debris:

> Rep. Ken Hechler, D-W.Va., said a decision Wednesday by the U.S. Court of Appeals that gives the go-ahead for the construction of the Blue Ridge power project on the New River is "ridiculous."

Just clearing away the clutter couldn't salvage that opener. You have to exhume an angle from the next-to-last graf of the story:

> Rep. Ken Hechler says people in West Virginia and two other states will mobilize to protect the New River after Wednesday's "ridiculous" court decision approving the Blue Ridge power project.

Try Writing "Visually"

How do you avoid mumblers? Start by being specific and succinct. Don't let subsidiary detail get in the way. Instead, select details that the reader can see. I call it visual writing. Like this:

> MADISON, Wis. (AP) — State Sen. Clifford "Tiny" Krueger eased his 300-pound frame into a witness chair Friday and said fat people should not be barred from adopting children.

That little gem draws the reader right into the story. Here's another, which tells virtually the whole story in two short sentences:

> MIAMI (AP) — Bill Cashman, a fireman, says he didn't mind posing nude for a centerfold in a magazine for women who like men. But he has a $2 million objection to use of the picture by a magazine for men who like men.

Want to read on? Of course. And who could resist wanting to read more after this lead?

> MARIETTA, Ohio (AP) — His work done, his children grown, his age past 80, his days of toil to get ahead well behind, George Oakes nonetheless sat down one day and built a better mousetrap.

That last example demonstrates a useful trick in the art of writing, especially the writing of effective leads. It is this. Very often, as in this sentence, the word you want to emphasize most comes at the end.

What's the Difference?

The real key to lifting your lead out of the humdrum is to ask yourself what, about this particular story, is *different*.

Much of the news is repetitive: war, crime, disaster. The goal, both in the lead and in the rest of the story, is to stress those angles that are least like the routine of other stories in this class. Many times this special element is there and writers overlook it. By overlooking it, they deprive themselves of the chance to equip their lead with that small hook that engages the reader's interest.

For example:

> YOUNGSTOWN, Ohio — A car sliced through a crowded fast food restaurant at lunchtime Tuesday, officials said, killing two people and injuring six others.

Nothing wrong with that lead. Well, perhaps the attribution, *officials said,* could wait until the second paragraph since nothing in the story is in contention. In any case, a car smashing into a restaurant at lunchtime is news enough for a lead, you might say, and it is written clearly and succinctly.

But eight grafs into the story appears a tidbit of information from the coroner. The two who were killed were a husband and wife, ages 72 and 68, who had stopped "to have a sandwich before going to the funeral home down the street for the funeral of their son-in-law's uncle." Aha, the writer should have said, and written:

YOUNGSTOWN, Ohio — A car sliced through a fast food restaurant Tuesday, killing an elderly couple who had stopped for lunch on the way to a family member's funeral. Six other people were injured.

This account of a famous execution was written in 1917. It has endured because of the lead:

PARIS — Mata Hari, which is Javanese for Eye-of-the-Morning, is dead. She was shot as a spy by a firing squad of Zouaves at the Vincennes Barracks. She died facing death literally, for she refused to be blindfolded.

Sometimes that nugget of difference can be supplied by the writer. Be alert for such opportunities. This writer was not:

FRANKFORT, Ky. (AP) — Local school boards in Kentucky are being caught in the middle of a controversy over posting copies of the Ten Commandments in public school classrooms.

When the story arrived at the AP's General Desk in New York the lead was reshaped this way, taking advantage of a blessed opportunity:

FRANKFORT, Ky. (AP) — Thou shalt post the Ten Commandments on the classroom wall, says a 1978 Kentucky law. Thou shalt not, says the U.S. Supreme Court. Help! say confused local school boards.

Needless to say, cleverness demands caution. It is easy to slip over the line into questionable taste, or even silliness.

HARTFORD, Conn. — Hello, tree. There is good news and there is bad news for you today.

That's plain silly.

Beware Overloads

A common cause of cardiac arrest in leads is overloading — too many ideas, too much inconsequential detail.
Do the mechanics matter in this lead?

SAN FRANCISCO — Rank and file members of two Bay Area Rapid Transit unions voted Thursday night to authorize a strike call by an ad-hoc committee of labor groups negotiating with the transit agency.

Concentrate on the result:

SAN FRANCISCO — Two Bay Area Rapid Transit unions Thursday night authorized their negotiators to call a strike.

Attempting too much is courting failure. The spot news lead is not the place to fuss with complicated narrative and sequence; it will sprout a rash of direction arrows like *before, after, while, as* and *then* and leave the reader befuddled:

DES MOINES, Iowa — Surprised firemen came across 10 bodies — and *then* began looking for more — *as* they battled a blaze in a Des Moines store Sunday *after* officials said everyone had left the building safely.

The following lead is equally misbegotten:

"He was the boss and we just kind of guided him," said Maj. Joseph Ernst of the captor he and another police officer volunteered to be hostage of Saturday in exchange for four civilians held at gunpoint by a disgruntled neighbor.

Volunteered to be hostage of Saturday? The sentence totters from beginning to end. Moreover, it's a bad idea to start a lead with quotes unless they are striking. They seldom come strong enough for that. Simplified:

One of two police officers who volunteered on Saturday as hostages in exchange for four people held at gunpoint by a neighbor says, "He was the boss, and we just kind of guided him."

Next, another case against overloading and a case against the comma as well:

NEW YORK — Ballerina Maya Plisetskaya, for Americans probably the best-known dancer in the Bolshoi Ballet, isn't on the company's tour to New York, Chicago and Los Angeles, company artistic director Yuri Grigorovich explained Tuesday, "for the usual reasons."

It's a wonder the writer neglected to add the first nine bars from *Swan Lake*. All that's needed:

NEW YORK — The Bolshoi Ballet's artistic director said Tuesday that ballerina Maya Plisetskaya is skipping the company's American tour "for the usual reasons" — she felt like it.

The following lead is intelligible, but much too busy:

TEHRAN — The military government arrested the former head of Iran's secret police today and then sent tanks to Tehran's bazaar area as reports circulated that the opposition was mounting another mass demonstration today against the 37-year rule of Shah Mohammad Reza Pahlavi.

For a starter, we don't need the bit of background at the end of that interminable sentence. Even without it, it would go better in two sentences:

TEHRAN — The military government arrested the former chief of Iran's secret police today. Then it sent tanks to Tehran's bazaar area amid reports that the opposition was mounting another demonstration against the Shah.

Horse First, Then Cart

Leads that start with long subsidiary clauses marching ahead of the main idea are usually losers. The news is needlessly delayed:

WASHINGTON — Saying that the Soviet actions in Afghanistan left him no other choice, President Carter today ordered an embargo on grain shipments to the Soviet Union.

This should be:

WASHINGTON — President Carter today banned grain shipments to the Soviet Union. He said Russian actions in Afghanistan left no choice.

Another example:

With consumers continuing their stay away from showrooms and the general economy showing further signs of decline, automakers today announced a new wave of layoffs in plants here and elsewhere.

The layoffs are the hard news:

> Detroit automakers today announced new layoffs as car sales and the general economy continued to decline.

A short introductory phrase, on the other hand, is often effective:

> One wing afire, an Air Force plane made a successful emergency landing at . . .

The test is simple: Does the phrase help what follows or just get in the way?

Leads also suffer from the feebles in trying to encompass too many news elements, a normal risk in writing roundups. Most of the time, the writer should settle on one news point. He threw everything into the following:

> WASHINGTON — The world's shifting energy outlook is prompting concern about possible changes in global climate, a consumer group says changing U.S. policies could bring increased profits to major oil companies, and the President's Office of Management and Budget says the Energy Department is a mess.

So is that lead.

Often there's sound reason for starting a lead with the source — notably when the statement or action derives all its significance from the speaker or doer. Not much reason here:

> WASHINGTON — The General Accounting Office, an investigative branch of Congress, issued a report Tuesday recommending federal leadership . . .

Yes, yes, but what did it say?

> . . . to reduce the amount of low-level radioactive waste from nuclear plants.

Give priority to the news:

WASHINGTON — The federal government should push for reductions in low-level radioactive wastes from nuclear plants, the General Accounting Office recommended Tuesday.

The GAO, an investigative arm of Congress, issued a report . . .

Control Yourself

If you hold to the rule that good leads rarely exceed 25 to 30 words, you won't go wrong. With some writers, the tendency is to overstuff leads in proportion to the importance of the story. Big story, big lead. The opposite treatment is usually the correct one. Good writers are aware of the virtue of restraint. A lead by the AP's John Barbour:

Man landed on the moon, this day, Sunday, July 20, 1969.

On another notable date, April 14, 1865, the AP's Lawrence A. Gobright filed this lead, a model in any era:

WASHINGTON (AP) — The President was shot in a theater tonight and perhaps mortally wounded.

A Matter of Tension

A good lead is like a fiddle string, the product of the right tension. One detail too few or too many and the note will be off. An overstuffed lead pants and hisses, an underdone lead whispers, and there's a fine line between the two.

This one is clearly overstuffed:

PHILADELPHIA — Federal attorneys who say they fear the destruction of records related to their civil suit alleging Philadelphia officials condone police abuse "may be afflicted with paranoia," City Solicitor Sheldon Albert said Monday.

Getting to the point:

PHILADELPHIA — Federal attorneys who fear for the safety of records involved in a suit alleging abuse of police powers "may be afflicted with paranoia," City Solicitor Sheldon Albert said Monday.

In the following case, the impulse to pack the lead betrayed the writer into twaddle:

STARKE, Fla. — John Spenkelink, his room for legal maneuver almost gone, went to his death in the electric chair today after he was allowed final visits by his family and his minister.

The fact that he was executed makes his room for legal maneuver zero, not almost gone. Why drag it in? Better:

STARKE, Fla. — John Spenkelink went to his death in the electric chair today after visits from his family and his minister.

Action Speaks Louder

Earlier we discussed the power of action verbs. They matter even more in sentences promoted to a lead. Verbs like *moved, scheduled, expected, prepared,* which so often crop up in second-day leads, are anemic. See what the good choice of verbs does for these leads:

NEW YORK — To the last day, Americans *flocked* to the tall ships at berth, *clambered up* the treacherous gangplanks, *grasped* the huge wheels, and *fondled* the brass windlasses.

FRANKLINTON, La. — A tank truck carrying 7,000 gallons of gasoline *collided* with a car and *overturned* Monday, crushing the trucker to death and igniting a fire that *spread* 50-foot flames over two blocks.

This next one, too, is able to stretch the preferred wordage for leads by painting a vivid picture:

NAILA, West Germany — Eight East Germans, including four children, *floated* through the night skies over Germany and across the "death strip" border to the West on Sunday in a hot-air balloon *stitched* together from bits of nylon and bedsheets.

Pitfalls of Attribution

A common pitfall for the lead writer comes with attribution. Cattle may chew cud contentedly, but readers shouldn't be asked to digest the same bit of information several times within a few paragraphs. Such repetition is often the fault of clumsy structure, particularly in backing up or elaborating on the lead. Some writers have trouble introducing a new fact without swaddling it in information or phrases that have gone before. So double-decker leads result, the second or third graf saying much the same as the first:

> The American Medical Association will receive its own "checkup" — an investigation by the Federal Trade Commission.
> The FTC announced Tuesday that it will investigate the AMA to determine whether it has unlawfully restrained . . .

In many cases it just takes minor adjusting to avoid this. Try it this way:

> The American Medical Association will receive its own checkup — from the Federal Trade Commission.
> The FTC announced Tuesday that it will study whether the AMA has . . .

Here's a double-decker carried to extremes:

> When Howard Hughes was put aboard an air ambulance for the final flight of his aviation-oriented life, he looked "wasted" and "like a tired, wornout old person," the pilots said Monday.
> "He just looked like a tired, worn-out old person," said Jeff Abrams, co-pilot of the Lear jet on which Hughes, an aviation pioneer, died Monday while being rushed from Acapulco, Mexico, to Houston.
> Roger Sutton, pilot of the Gray Jet Air Ambulance Service of Fort Lauderdale, described Hughes as being emaciated, with a thin beard and long, grayish hair.
> "He was very wasted," said Sutton.

Having quoted the pilots in the first graf, the writer can't solve the problem of attribution without repeating everything. The solution, though, is easy:

> When Howard Hughes was put aboard an air ambulance for the

final flight of his aviation-oriented life, he looked 'like a tired, worn-out old person," co-pilot Jeff Abrams said.

Pilot Roger Sutton said Hughes had a thin beard and long grayish hair and appeared "very wasted."

Hughes died Monday aboard the Lear jet en route from Acapulco, Mexico, to Houston.

A vintage double-decker:

Half of the Philadelphia Art Museum's permanent galleries were closed Sunday because of a shortage of security guards.

Museum officials said they had to close part of the museum because the city had not provided money for about 100 additional guards.

In attributing and getting to the 100 guards, half the lead is repeated. Slight recasting moves the story along:

Half of the Philadelphia Art Museum's permanent galleries were closed Sunday because the city had failed to provide money for 100 more security guards, Director Edward Turner said.

Second-Cycle Woes

Overstuffing, double-decking and other fatal diseases are often encountered when the writer is struggling with that old nemesis, the second-cycle lead. Every reporter will eventually confront a second-cycle lead; for Associated Press reporters it is a part of the daily routine. Since phrases like "day before yesterday" are not in the vocabulary of leads, the problem arises in trying to make old news appear fresh. With no new development to come to the rescue, writers are left to their own resources.

This writer, reporting the day-old news that McGovern had fired his executive assistant, was up to the challenge:

WASHINGTON — Sen. George McGovern remembers what it's like to fight an uphill battle in the Democratic presidential primaries and then find party leaders still struggling to deny him the nomination.

McGovern resented it when it happened to him in 1972. And he says he doesn't want any part of a similar effort to thwart Democratic frontrunner Jimmy Carter in 1976 — despite the fact that Carter was one of the politicians who sought to block McGovern four years ago.

So on Monday, McGovern fired his executive assistant . . .

This writer found his own resources wanting:

LAS VEGAS, Nev. — Arson investigators sifted through the rubble of a spectacular fire Sunday that leveled most of a shopping center just off the heart of the glittering Las Vegas strip.

The blaze that began Saturday night destroyed . . .

Leads that report investigators (or grim-faced rescue workers, or weary homeowners) *sifting through the rubble* or *poking through the debris* are written by writers wallowing through the clichés and tossing in the towel. A narrative or anecdotal lead would be more interesting than those overworked rescue workers in disaster stories: *Most families in Smithtown were having supper when the sirens sounded. In the next few minutes . . .*

Self-respecting writers will find ways to avoid those second-cycle clichés. This one did:

LAKEHURST, N.J. — Karl Thomas is drifting over the Atlantic Ocean today in his try to become the first person to reach Europe by balloon from the United States.

After days of delay because of unfavorable weather, the 27-year-old pilot from Troy, Mich., caught a strong westerly breeze about 9 a.m. Friday and sailed away . . .

No new developments here, but this resourceful writer made use of information at hand:

SAN RAFAEL, Calif. — The state of California spent 16 months and more than $2 million to convict three men who were already imprisoned, two with life sentences.

Three of the San Quentin Six were found guilty Thursday . . .

That lead was written at the end of a trial. Reporters covering the early stages of a trial face tougher problems. Trials have moments of high drama, but the stage of jury selection is not among them. Yawning reporters often refer to it as the *long, tedious process* of seating a jury, but the process is far from tedious to lawyers and defendants, whose minds are on other matters than providing entertainment.

Terrible leads are often written during that phase: *Three more jurors were tentatively seated Thursday as the trial entered its fifth day,* which is later topped with a lead that has two more jurors chosen.

Obviously, the number of jurors chosen must be reported. Probably the best way to handle it is to mention high up that jury-selection is continuing, and then, in the middle of your story, run a paragraph that by such and such a time X number of jurors had been picked. You can update the figures without changing the lead or breaking the continuity of the story.

Meantime, work on a more interesting angle. For example:

> MINEOLA, N.Y. (AP) — Prospective jurors in the trial of a doctor charged with the "mercy killing" of a dying cancer patient were closely questioned about their religious beliefs and attitudes toward the medical profession.

Despite all the dying, that lead has a semblance of life. The numbers (*Eight jurors have been seated . . .*) fell into place later in the story.

Watch the Bouncing Ball

While on the subject of covering the courts, beware another snare that plagues this special field of reporting. Court rulings, administrative decisions and the like are usually couched in technicalities and legalese, and leads don't always simplify these terms the way they should. Here's an example:

A federal judge refused Wednesday to issue a temporary injunction halting a union ratification vote on the binding arbitration contract handed down last week for the American Postal Workers union and the U.S. Postal Service.

Anybody care to tell a struggling reader what happened? Well, it was like this. The judge wouldn't block the vote on a contract. Moreoever, since the contract resulted from binding arbitration — meaning the union members weren't free to accept or reject it — the vote could have no effect on it. They were going through motions, that's all. So:

A federal judge refused Wednesday to block a vote by postal workers on a new contract even though the vote would be pointless except as a gesture.

AP Executive Editor Lou Boccardi calls this turgidity in court coverage "tennis-ball writing." Here's another example of it:

WASHINGTON — The U.S. Court of Appeals agreed Wednesday to review a lower court order that found the Nuclear Regulatory Commission in contempt of court for violating an order to hold open budget meetings.

Boccardi's comment in his writing bulletin, *Prose and Cons*:

"The problem here is that we treat the reader's mind like a tennis ball to be whacked back and forth across the net. Agreed to review. Bam! Contempt of court. Bam! For violating an order. Bam! To hold open meetings. Bam! You can almost see the ball flying back and forth. It's just too much. You cure it by just stepping back and asking yourself, 'What really happened here?' " This happened:

WASHINGTON — The U.S. Court of Appeals agreed Wednesday to review a contempt finding against the Nuclear Regulatory Commission for holding a closed meeting.

Reporters indulge in tennis-ball writing and legal jargon because they don't quite trust themselves to tell in a straightforward way what's going on. By sticking to the legal terms, they play it safe. Here's an example of playing it so safe the story is unintelligible:

> RICHMOND, Va. — Attorney General Andrew P. Miller says a juvenile who in a juvenile or domestic relations court is convicted of and receives a sentence for what, if committed by an adult, would be a misdemeanor or a felony cannot be housed with adult prisoners in prisons or jails.
>
> In an opinion released Monday, Miller said it would be a violation of state law to incarcerate juveniles in such a manner unless the incarceration is mainly for the purpose of pre-trial detention or if the juvenile is certified to a circuit court and tried as an adult.

That's a legal tennis match to boggle the mind. In English, I presume it would mean this:

> RICHMOND, Va. — A youthful offender receiving a prison sentence in a juvenile or domestic relations court cannot be jailed with adult prisoners, the attorney general has ruled.
>
> Placing him with adult inmates would violate state law unless it's for pre-trial detention or unless he's been tried in a circuit court.

Legalistic Leads

In covering police and court stories, there is sometimes legitimate use in the lead for otherwise cumbersome or legalistic words and phrases. One of these is *in connection with* in stories about people who are questioned or arrested or sought for a crime with which they haven't been charged. But there's absolutely no warrant for using it *after* a man has been charged (say what he was charged with) or after he's been sentenced or pronounced guilty. Some reporters are so afflicted with the legal shakes that you can read:

> Joseph Smith was scheduled Monday to be sentenced in connection with the Smithtown murder after a jury convicted him . . .

Another abused word is *suspect*. It's seldom a very good word to use in any case; if somebody's questioned, or wanted for questioning, let those facts speak for themselves. If the authorities declare somebody to be *a prime suspect* in a case, so be it; quote them. It is ridiculous in crime stories, however, to refer to unknown but indubitable culprits as *suspects,* because, while nobody knows their names, they're the ones who have done it:

> Two suspects held up a jewelry store at 14th and Main today, tying up a clerk and rifling several display cases before escaping.

The Time Element

A special problem with leads is comparatively recent, the shift to the use of the day of the week. *Today* and *yesterday* fit gracefully into leads. Thursday and Friday are often balky.

As a rule, put the time element after the verb unless the day of the week can be read as the object of the verb or is awkward in other ways, producing oddities. A Washington story reports that Congress *postponed Wednesday.* In New York, a top federal mediator *sought Thursday,* presumably without finding it. A story begins, *Middlesex Superior Court Judge Henry Chielinsky Thursday . . .*

Some writers stick *on* before the day, interrupting the succession of capital letters, but this is generally considered a non-solution, adding a word with little gain.

There's no ready formula. You must use your ear as well as your eye. How does it sound? Some leads read well with the day of the week, others don't. When it's cumbersome no matter where you try to shoehorn the word into a sentence, drop the day to the second paragraph, where it often fits quite naturally. You do *not* have to put the time element in every lead, either AMs or PMs.

Wrestling with such small details, and with many larger matters of technique, may be joyless, but in leads every word must count. Some of the improvements suggested in the examples of clumsy leads doubtless could have been improved further. But the attempts all led in one direction: toward a lean, uncluttered sentence, toward the news itself rather than its attendant lords, toward logical order of thought, toward concrete and specific language. Those are the goals.

TONE:
The Inner Music
of Words

4

After you've squared away your lead, herded your paragraphs into place, and swept up the small verbal debris, lend an ear. Does your copy sound conversational or stilted? Pompous or overly breezy? Formal or relaxed?

Tone ultimately determines whether your reader is pleased or not. Sentence structure has something to do with it, but tone is primarily generated by the choice of words. Plain, short, familiar words produce one distinct tone; fancy polysyllables another.

And then there are the "insides" of words. Many words have a special inner music — clusters of associations and images that roost just below the surface.

House, home, residence and *domicile* all denote the same thing, but only a tone-deaf writer (which should be a contradiction in terms) would use them interchangeably, regardless of context. *The old couple lived in a cozy residence* rings false; but there's nothing wrong with *they changed their residence frequently.*

Emulate, copy and *ape* refer to the same activity, but you wouldn't write that a worthy novice was *aping* a saint. You'd use *emulate,* because it has honorable connotations, while *copy* suggests a mindless, mechanical process and *ape* has contemptuous overtones.

A word utterly misused destroys tone with a primal scream:

> WASHINGTON — A half-hour later, a solemn-faced Reagan walked to the front door of the White House and, standing with his wife, Nancy, at the North Portico, expressed his *remorse*.

What Reagan was doing was expressing his sorrow, regret or anger over the assassination of Anwar Sadat. Only the killers could have expressed remorse (sorrow or guilt for one's own wrongdoing).

This, of course, was an aberration. Most questions of tone are subtler. Consider these passages:

> But long-term positive aspects of the revolutionary process far transcended initial defects. The American Revolution was dynamic, not static, and took it upon itself to amend and improve imperfections in its structure.

> The world has a stern neighborhood cop again. That was the point President Reagan wanted to make when he ordered America's 6th Fleet to sail into a stretch of sea arbitrarily claimed by Colonel Khadafy's Libya and respected as a no-go by former President Carter. The Libyans fell for it, giving America a chance to wield its night stick.

The first passage is from a newspaper, the second from a magazine. Both passages deal with serious subjects and both are clear, but they are octaves apart in tone. One is weighed down by ponderous abstract words of a distinctly academic flavor; you might say it's static, not dynamic. The other is almost conversational, skipping along on plain words and homely analogies.

Avoid Sudden Shifts

Tone need not be uniform, but sudden shifts are disconcerting, and a mixture of disparate tones grates like chalk on a slate.

Charles Dickens makes use of this effect with his immortal Mr. Micawber, whose passion for ornate language is happily tempered by his impulse to self-correction:

> Under the impression that your peregrinations in this Metropolis have not yet been extensive, and you might have difficulty in penetrating the arena of the modern Babylon . . . *In short, that you might get lost . . .*

Again and again Mr. Micawber, soaring, abruptly pulls himself back to earth. That's the side of him news writers should emulate.

Tone can go wrong in many ways besides turning pompous. It can, for example, become gushy, like the language you find in much advertising and promotion copy, in certain magazines and newspaper sections.

Words that usually signal gush are many, including *fabulous, tremendous, superb, unique, exquisite, gorgeous, fantastic, enchanting, incredible, glamorous* and the like. Public relations handouts are often gushers, and too much of that breathless verbiage slips through:

> Officials of the cable company said the *long-awaited* unveiling of the system will occur June 27, *ushering in a fabulous new viewing era.* . . .

The system will start operation June 27 says it all.

> The ship is *posh* from stem to stern, a floating *lap of luxury*, with *exquisite* food and a whirl of activities that keeps cruise passengers *tingling*.

It must be uncomfortable to float in a lapful of luxury, fabulous or otherwise. No wonder the passengers tingle.

A gushy lead:

> If John Smith had turned his energy and enthusiasm toward financially profitable pursuits, *the Hunt brothers might have a rival. Instead,* he gave up fame and fortune (or at least a financially secure existence) for the sake of children he had never met.

The reader is instantly skeptical. A rival for the Hunts? A man few of them have heard of giving up fame and fortune? The skepticism proves well-founded. The story is about a social worker who held some state jobs, quit, and started a privately funded program for street kids. That's nice, but insufficient for the flushed lead.

We Are Not Amused

Never treat death, pain and suffering — human or animal — lightly or humorously. The following story takes a persistently wrong tone:

So, you think you've got problems? Wait till you hear the story of Chuh-Chuh the shih-tzu from Howard Beach.

Sour Note 1: The lead asks the reader to identify with a dog.

The dog's owners filed for $5.1 million damages yesterday in state Supreme Court, claiming they had suffered distress and psychological pain, while the dog suffered prolonged pain following castration by a veterinarian. Chuh-Chuh died in early August, nine days after the operation.

Sour Note 2: Details of animal's suffering and owners' grief make flippant lead doubly dubious.

The veterinarian said the owners' attorney, Harry L. Lipsig, had a bark that is worse than his bite. Dr. Donald Wirth of the Lefferts Dog and Cat Hospital denied that he was responsible for the death of Chuh-Chuh.

Sour Note 3: More limp flippancy. Did the vet really say that?

"What the hell are they suing me for?" he said. "A lot of people have strong attachments to their pets. But this is outrageous. Shih-tzus are nice little dogs that cost about $300."

Sour Note 4: "What the hell" quote is pointless.

Lipsig said, "There is the pain and suffering the poor creature went through. He was practically a member of the family."

Some readers might be amused by this treatment, but a great many more would put on a long face.

For reasons of tone, likewise, don't refer to serious accidents as *mishaps*. A man twisting his ankle stepping off a curb has a mishap; if a car hits him and he's paralyzed from the waist down, it's an accident. The word *incident* also suggests something of small consequence, a peripheral event — say a picket line scuffle. A shootout in which several are hurt or killed is more than an *incident*.

Beware the Personal Touch

Addressing readers directly makes for a pleasantly personal tone in stories that lend themselves to this approach. But beware of casting readers in roles they can't readily envision for themselves, and don't link them to something disagreeable, as the *you* lead of the dog story did.

If you've ever struggled with a garden full of weeds is a situation ordinary enough so that readers, non-gardeners included, have no trouble seeing themselves that way. But if you write, *If you've ever thought about biting the head off a live chicken,* the personal note turns bizarre and the reader's response will be at best muted.

The following lead is lively and clever in that it mimics the writing style of the subject, a book author. But unless you are aware of that, it demands too much willingness to pretend:

> NEW YORK — You are practicing law in New York, supporting a family and paying the bills. But in your spare time, you are also writing children's books — in longhand, in your battered spiral notebook.
> What do you do?
> If you choose to remain a lawyer, this is the end of your story. But if you are Edward Packard, you chuck the law career.. . .

Somewhere soon in this list of particulars, the *you* is apt to stir uneasily and ask, *Who, me?*

Busy, Busy, Busy

The following is a dramatic story clearly and simply told, but overuse of "loud" words produces a racket:

> A *blazing* fire broke out on the 47th floor of a Lower Manhattan skyscraper today, threatening to turn it into a *towering inferno*.
> Seven persons were injured — at least one critically — and two others were reported missing, the Fire Department said.
> Hundreds — many of whom had been eating in a *posh* restaurant — fled the building.
> Traffic on Lower Broadway was brought to a *complete* halt.
> An unidentified cleaning man who was riding the freight elevator was injured when the elevator opened on the 47th floor.
> Flames *exploded* and *blasted* him in the face.
> "His body was ignited head to foot," a witness said.

This is pretty busy. The fire is *blazing*, the restaurant *posh*, traffic doesn't just come to a halt but a *complete* halt, the inferno that's merely threatened in the first paragraph becomes fact by the fifth, flames explode *and* blast. (A reader might ask if that witness was standing in the *inferno*.)

Don't Be Absurd

The writer of the following passage is flirting with absurdity from the start and finally embraces it. The story concerned a sex education program for the very, very young. The exuberant tone adds to the difficulty of keeping a straight face:

> The child picked up the plastic model of a uterus, examined it closely and announced: "This looks like a fwog."
> The resemblance was remote, but his parents were nonetheless happy. They had begun a dialogue with their 3-year-old son that they hoped would continue through his childhood and adolescence.

The tone shuttles between the pompous and the cutesy and collapses with the unlikely suggestion of a serious dialogue with a 3-year-old.

Since the writer intended readers to take the project seriously, he would have done better to flatten out the passage, perhaps like this:

> The child picked up the plastic uterus and said it looked like a frog. For the parents, it was the start of teaching their 3-year-old something about the facts of life. They want him to continue to discuss the subject with them freely through childhood and adolescence.

A far more subtle example is offered by a fine story that has perfect pitch except for two notes slightly off key. The writer is telling it through the youngsters' experiences, and the simple style is in tune and rhythm:

> When 10-year-old Midaglia Roman learned that she wasn't promoted with her fourth grade class this year, she cried all the way home.
> Today, Midaglia got her second chance. "I'd rather be here," the pretty, big-eyed girl said as she sat with about 30 others in a warm classroom at Public School 34, where the Board of Education is running a special summer school for students who were "left back" under a get-tough policy.

The story continues in this vein until:

> Many, like Midaglia, will have a final try at the reading test when it's given again Aug. 14. They hope to *hone their skills* sufficiently in the coming week so they can go on with their class.

And in a later paragraph:

> But some students were less happy about the *intrusion on their summer plans*.

This story reads well as it stands. But the writer has been so attentive to keeping the tone modulated to youngsters' ways of thinking that the phrases *honed their skills* and *intrusion on their summer plans* add a sudden touch of stuffiness. *Brush up on their reading* and *missing out on some summer fun* might have been more consistent.

Dealing With Motive

Nuances like this may largely belong to the upper reaches of feature writing, but our next examples deal with handling motive, which is very much a problem of straight news.

Writers sometimes feel the urge to judge a newsmaker's motive because it may seem part of the whole truth of a story. But this is tricky business. For one thing, unless you read minds you can't be sure. For another, motives are often mixed, to the point where the actor himself is unclear about them.

Following are three ways of dealing with motive — one wrong, the second better but still questionable, the third right.

1. Wrong:

> LOS ANGELES — For the second time in a week, Gov. Edmund G. Brown Jr. yesterday appeared to be courting the Jewish vote for an expected 1982 Senate campaign as he attacked the planned sale of $8.5 billion in arms to Saudi Arabia.

As AP Executive Editor Lou Boccardi commented on this one in his newsletter *Prose and Cons*:

"We can't be so naive that we think governors speak without considering the political effects of what they say.

But we also can't say the man is simply appealing for votes rather than expressing views truly held. It's clumsy and does him a disservice."

2. Better, but still wide of the mark:

> AUSTIN, Texas — Land Commissioner Bob Armstrong announced the "good news" today that the Permanent School fund had reached $3 billion, then admitted he was thinking about running for governor.

The writer doesn't say so outright, but the tone is unmistakable and the announcement is linked to political motive.

3. The right way:

> WASHINGTON — The sponsor of a bill to ease air pollution standards says the best way to clean air is to encourage people to junk their old cars and buy new ones.
> "Each time a 1970 Impala is junked and a 1981 Chevette is added to the American fleet, the air gets cleaner," said Rep. Bob Traxler, D-Mich., sponsor of the industry-backed bill.

Down in the story is this paragraph:

> Traxler and Ellis represent districts where auto manufacturing is the dominant industry.

This is pertinent background, played straight. No winks, sneers, or nudges. The speaker has his say and the reader is given the facts objectively.

No Hints, Please

Matters of tone and motive loom large also in investigative stories where writers sometimes resort to hints and innuendoes and suggestive arrangements of damaging detail to establish what the evidence itself fails to demonstrate:

> *Incredibly*, Smith did not report his failure to file the returns until eight *long* years later . . .

> In another of those *remarkable "coincidences,"* the records were

damaged by a *convenient* fire four days before the subpoena arrived. *Of course* the defendants claimed they hadn't known the records were being sought.

The young prosecutor said *candidly* he had all but given up on the case. Doe, asked about the turn of events, withdrew once again into a *sullen* "no comment."

This tone is editorial, snide and, in essence, prosecutorial. And, paradoxically, it is usually much less effective than factual, even detached statement. If you have solid information logically marshalled, the readers will draw their own inferences, without the aid of zingers.

They will be the more readily persuaded the less you resort to emotive words, small injections of opinion, knowing winks and lopsided selection of details. The less you comment or characterize, the better. An obvious attempt to push readers toward a foreshadowed conclusion is self-defeating; many resist such ham-handed pressure tactics. And, of course, there's the matter of objectivity, as crucial in investigative as any other form of reporting.

Perhaps there's a mindset to investigative reporting that sometimes betrays writers into the prosecutorial tone. Gene Roberts, executive editor of the *Philadelphia Inquirer*, which has a notable record of major investigative projects, touched on it in a discussion at an Associated Press Managing Editors convention.

"I think where many papers go astray in trying to do alleged investigative reporting is in defining it as unearthing criminals," he said. "This immediately casts the reporters as cops rather than as gatherers of information. Society will get along quite well without newsrooms that view themselves as police forces."

Roberts doesn't even like the word "investigative," and on the *Inquirer* "we stay away from the term investigative stories in favor of terms like 'takeouts' and 'project pieces.' "

He added, "The finest reporting, short or long, is always investigative in that it digs and digs and digs. The finest writing is almost by definition explanatory in that it puts things so vividly, so compellingly, that readers see and understand."

Watch It, Kiddo

An informal, relaxed tone appeals to most people, but avoid excessive colloquialism and forced heartiness; don't get too chummy with your readers. It's an affectation and a form of writing down:

> The board of directors, after a daylong wrangle, lowered the boom on Smith. He was the third top honcho of the corporation to get the ax in as many years.

This is painful stuff, not because it offends the majesty of a corporation, but because backslapping breeziness has no place in a serious story.

A story backgrounding the events in Iran strikes a similar wrong note:

> The late Shah, who *got kicked out* of the country in . . .
> But he was forced into wandering when country after country *sent him packing*.

A third specimen:

> Most members of Congress are expressing dismay and skepticism over President Carter's shakeup, with one congressional leader saying the president had *blown* whatever gains he made with the new initiatives on the energy front.

Blown jars in this otherwise formal sentence. Since the writer was paraphrasing — the word *blown* doesn't appear in the direct quotes at all — *spoiled* would have been a better choice.

Referring to news subjects by first name also carries informality too far. It's most often practiced on entertainment figures, athletes and other celebrities. The reporter is showing off a familiarity that's usually spurious, and the reader senses it.

It's different in writing about youngsters, when the use of the last name seems forced — up to age 15, anyway. Consistent use of the first name sounds more natural here. And avoid references like *the Jones boy* or *the Smith woman*, which are simply rude.

Euphemism: Use and Misuse

With all cultural indicators in our society pointing to the more explicit, "genteelism" — the refined tone that dotes on overly polite words and euphemisms — has been fading from daily journalism, though it still survives.

It survives in part because of jargon, which has invaded all parts of the language and among other defacements substitutes abstractions and euphemism for plain words: *disadvantaged* for the poor, *underachievers* for the lazy or unwilling or downright mean, *senior citizens* for the elderly or old, *interact* for mingle with or make friends, *disturbed* for the mentally ill or violent, and many more.

Blather imported from the social sciences is a rich tributary to this variant of genteelism. Government is another fertile source. A fine example bowing in lately is *revenue enhancement*, much more agreeable than *tax increase*.

Other genteelisms, best avoided, are *mortician* for undertaker, *interment* for burial, *casket* for coffin, *lady* for woman, and *expecting* for pregnant. Even *pass away* for die still survives, and one Midwestern paper in a wedding story had the couple *motoring to their honeymoon haven*, a delightful archaism and most genteel.

All this is not to rule out euphemism entirely. We use it legitimately to avoid vulgarity or to soften something innately disgusting. Unlike genteelism, that is genuine politeness to the reader. As Theodore Bernstein mildly put it in

The Careful Writer, "It may be preferable to write that a man and a woman 'spent the night together' than to set forth in detail how they spent it."

Euphemism is objectionable only when used to doll up an emotionally stark but otherwise unexceptional fact of the human condition.

There's a directly musical aspect of tone that also deserves attention in news writing — those inadvertent collisions of syllables and sounds that cause readers pause (as cause/pause does in this sentence). A string of words ending in 'shun, for example, grates: *The organization gave attention to the situation. That fact doesn't detract from the act* is another disturbing sequence. A man innocently named Redding creates tiny havoc: *Redding, reading from his prepared text.* Such unlucky combinations, which are easily remedied, create a buzzing in the reader's head that distracts from the business at hand.

Simplicity Will Do

Tone, as we have seen, varies widely, depending on the story, the subject, the skill of writers, the passions of copy desks, and the preferences of editors. Tone is not the same at *The Wall Street Journal, The New York Times,* the *New York Post* and the *Los Angeles Times.*

By and large, though, the most effective journalistic tone in the '80s would seem to be the plain and unadorned. That at least is the premise of this book. It is a tone that speaks to readers, not at them, that explains, but doesn't lecture — conversational, perhaps, but correct, never shrill and jazzed up.

Here's an example of the plain tone, taken from a story by AP Special Correspondent Jules Loh about the shooting of the town bully, the sort of story that often lures writers with a less disciplined ear into a rat-tat-tat, melodramatic style:

> He wasn't a street brawler. He was specific. He struck fear in your soul by staring you down, flashing a gun, occasionally using it. If you were his prey for today he stalked you. He glared at you in silence and when he spoke it was in a slow whisper. Chilling.
>
> He was born on a farm just outside of town. When he was a boy he fell off a hay wagon, requiring a steel plate to be implanted in his head. Some wondered if that was what made him so mean.
>
> This is a small town: 440 people, filling station, bank, post office, tavern, blacktop street, grain elevator. Beyond lie rolling meadows, ripening corn, redwing blackbirds, fat cattle, windmills and silos, a scene off a Sweet Lassy feed calendar.
>
> Ken McElroy jarred that pastoral serenity. So it is with outspoken relief that the citizens of Nodaway County now speak of him in the past tense. He is dead. The fear he brought them, though, still lingers in a new, unexpected form. . . .

Whatever gradations of tone you adopt, there can be no doubt about its importance for the writer. Barbara Tuchman, the historian, whose vivid prose combined with scholarship has made her books bestsellers, says in an essay on her craft:

"One learns to write by the practice thereof. After seven years' apprenticeship in journalism I have discovered that an essential element for good writing is a good ear. One must listen to the sound of one's own prose. This, I think, is one of the failures of much American writing. Too many writers do not listen to the sound of their own prose."

So listen.

PITFALLS: Attributive Verbs and Loaded Words

5

Among attributive verbs, *said* usually says it best. It's short, clear, neutral and unfailingly accurate, a verb for all seasons.

You'll need substitutes occasionally to avoid monotony, but be careful; they are not synonyms of *said,* not even — especially not — *stated* or *declared.*

Each attributive carries its own shade of meaning and must fit your context, a requirement remarkably often overlooked. *"Shut up," he explained,* is a fiction writer tongue in cheek. *"The sun rises every day," she recalled,* is a news writer foot in mouth.

Attributives kindle a craving for elegance in misguided souls, who reach for archaisms like *averred* or *innovate.* One newspaper rolled its own attributive, with shaky results: *"The costs were rather higher than we anticipated," she assessed.*

Editors and writers survive who consider the repetition of an attributive verb within a 500-word radius a disgrace: Seen in print was a chaste initial *said* followed by *asserted, averred, proclaimed, avowed, propounded* and *opined.*

The mounting suspense in following such a gaudy series was more gripping than the story.

Let's consider the behavior of some widely used attributive verbs, listed in rough order of their usefulness:

Went on	Insisted	Cautioned	Predicted
Continued	Maintained	Explained	
Added	Complained	Recalled	

The words in the first column are plain and as neutral as *said*. The others are simply descriptive; just make sure they fit the circumstances.

The following can be hazardous:

| Pointed out | Warned | Claimed |
| Noted | Charged | |

To say that a speaker *points out* something invests it with an aura of fact. The reader mentally supplies ". . . the fact that" after the verb. This means that *point out* can have editorial nuances: *"The Democrats have seldom done this nation much good," the mayor pointed out* seems to subscribe to the mayor's verdict. When there's no such risk, confine *pointed out* to instances when a speaker calls attention to something that might otherwise be overlooked: *"The police weren't legally required to use a warrant in this case," the attorney general pointed out.*

Noted has similar connotations of fact and is even duller than *pointed out.*

Warned should be confined to quotes that point to genuine danger. Avoid lending credence to rhetorical overkill: *"A Republican victory will mean the end of civilization as we know it," the candidate warned.*

Charged is best left to legal contexts: *"The company has willfully broken the public trust," the attorney general charged.* Don't use the word when casual criticism or mild complaints are involved: *"Some employees are stretching their coffee breaks to unconscionable lengths," the director charged.*

Claimed is a far remove from the neutral *said.* For reasons to be cautious, see the discussion of *claim* below.

The following attributives are widely misused.

Asserted	Remarked
Stated	Commented
Declared	Observed

Asserted, stated, declared are often indiscriminately used for *said.* All are stronger and much more formal. To *assert* means to put forward an opinion or position strongly held. When that's done, the statement will speak for itself without benefit of that stiff *asserted. Stated* shouldn't be used at all; it is the instant mark of a wooden writer. (It fits if you're quoting from a deposition, but still looks dusty.) You *declare* a war, an emergency or martial law; the verb is too ponderous for most quotes.

Remarked applies to casual statements only: *"It's a fine day," he remarked.* Not: *"Unless the Soviet Union withdraws from Afghanistan, our relations will continue on the present level," the spokesman remarked.*

Commented also connotes the offhand, incidental, expressing a personal reaction or attitude: *"This is hardly his best work," the principal commented.*

Observed is close in meaning to *remarked* and *commented,* but less conversational in tone and therefore less desirable.

All the following keep cropping up in newsprint, which is regrettable:

Avowed	Exclaimed
Averred	Quipped
Opined	Snapped

Avowed involves a strong moral commitment and is almost always overly dramatic. Its cousin, *vowed,* suggests a solemn oath, possibly sealed with blood from an index finger. *Promised* and *pledged* are invariably better.

Averred and *opined* should be relegated to Gothic novels or specialists in musty prose. *Exclaimed* usually underscores something that doesn't need underscoring.

Quipped is pointless when a real quip is quoted; too often the writer applies it to a lame remark that lacks bite.

A person may possibly *snap* one word, but only a Doberman can snap a sentence.

This last attributive brings us to applied physiology. Never use verbs denoting non-verbal processes as attributives, like *smiled, wept, laughed.* You don't smile words; you say them, smiling. *"I'm fond of him," she smiled,* is no less absurd than *"I'm very hot this morning," he radiated.*

Beware Loaded Words

It's the business of writers to say what they intend to say, neither more nor less, but sometimes by using certain words they carelessly impart values and judgments in stories where these don't belong.

Take reform. Reform is good by definition. The word means "to make better by removing faults or defects."

That's why politicians, lawmakers and partisans of every hue love to attach the word to the programs they're pushing.

But one person's reform is another's calamity. One side describes as *abortion law reform* a measure that the other side still considers a sanction of murder. A *tax reform bill* that leaves half the electorate fuming will be deemed an improvement only by the other half.

So unless you're dealing with changes that the vast majority of reasonable citizens regard as beneficial, you had better steer clear of calling them a reform on your own. Call them changes or revisions. If *reform* appears in the title of a bill or program that annoys as many as it pleases, make clear that *reform* is what the sponsors call it, not you.

Here are some other words to watch:

Admit, as in admitting a crime, implies yielding reluctantly under pressure. *The company chairman admitted that interest rates had not been factored into production estimates* suggests that he came clean after an astute reporter put the thumbscrews to him. In fact, he volunteered the information. Use *said.*

Bureaucrat. A slighting term for *official, civil servant, government employee.*

Candidly, frankly. The defense attorney said frankly that his case rested on a single witness. How do you know he was frank? Why not let statements speak for themselves, without such comments?

Claim is not a synonym for *say, assert* or *argue.* You claim a (disputed) right. In a sentence like *the policeman claimed that he saw the gun* the verb casts doubt on his assertion. Use it only when that's what you intend to do. The

word is used precisely in this sentence: *The company lawyers claimed that the patents extended to fast-film paper
as well.* There's doubt, to be resolved in court. For the same
reason, *"I'm a better singer than most of the younger per-
formers," the diva claimed,* is sensible usage. But *"I've
been in the Metropolitan Opera for 23 years," she claimed,*
is silly if she made a factual statement.

Loophole. Like *scheme* or *scheming,* it has connotations
of sly, devious, perhaps unethical proceedings. That's not
the case when taxpayers take advantage of such breaks as
the tax laws afford them. On the other hand, it's fair to
write of a loophole when a lawyer discovers a way out of a
contract due to an oversight that's plainly counter to the intent and purpose of the agreement.

Only. Even this little worm can turn: *Only five of the
nine administration measures got off the ground* belittles
through that *only.*

Scheme. That's just not another word for *plan,* just as
schemer isn't the same as *planner.* A *scheme* suggests
something shifty. That's not what the writer wanted to
imply in, *American Airlines disclosed a scheme to lure
new customers.*

Straightforward, steadfast. Characterizations that
imply approval, just as *stubborn* implies disapproval. Some
will consider the president's holding to his course as steadfast, others as stubborn.

This doesn't suggest, of course, that these words should
never be used. It's merely a caution to use them carefully,
with full regard for what the words imply.

QUOTES: Your Words or Mine?

6

News, to a remarkable degree, is what people say and how they say it — as actors in events, kibitzers, witnesses, informants, as movers and shakers and as the moved and the shaken. The chatter is incessant. So are the newswriter's efforts to distill useful quotes* from it.

Quotes, as even novices quickly realize, are indispensable. They lend authenticity. They put readers in touch with people as directly as print can manage it. A story of any length that lacks quotes is as barren as a lunar landscape.

In his book, *The Craft of Interviewing*, Tom Brady extols quotes as "those brief, brilliant bursts of life." Ideally, that's what they are. Unfortunately, though, many quotes are neither brief nor brilliant but lifeless and verbose.

This isn't necessarily the newswriter's fault. When people don't scintillate, you won't get scintillating quotes. But you can be selective about what you use. Too many writers

---

* — *Quotation* is, of course, the preferred noun form, but *quote* has been widely accepted, and is suitable in a journalistic context.

seem to assume that quotation marks, by themselves, can transform a grunt into a great fugue. *Smith said he accepted the job because it represented a "challenge."*) They help not at all.

In leisurely interviews and other setpieces, skilled reporters can patiently cast their lines until a few gaudy fish rise to the bait. In the hot pursuit of ordinary news, there's much less opportunity for that. Quotes are often snatched on the run: A hasty comment from a harassed lawyer, a cop's police blotter prose, the handful of dust stirred up by a bureaucrat scuttling for cover under a barrage of words.

All you can do with the stuff, by way of direct quotes, is to take it or leave it. Like other facts, quotes are not subject to revision. Once words are enclosed by quotation marks, they must be what the source said. Attempts to "improve" that by reshuffling or even changing words are high crimes and misdemeanors. The furthest you can go is to fix minor grammatical errors and omit pure padding or meaningless repetition.

When to Quote?

Under these constraints, the art of handling quotes comes down to knowing when to quote, when to paraphrase, when to forget the whole thing. Sometimes the choice is simple. When the Rev. Lester Roloff publicly defied Texas officials who threatened to close down his home for wayward girls, he intoned:* "It may be in the ninth inning and we may be behind in the score, but I see my bases loaded and Jesus Christ coming to bat."

Most writers, major and minor leaguers, would hit that fat pitch out of the ballpark. Most quotes aren't nearly so

---

* — With reference to the discussion of verbs in the preceding chapter, is it agreed that *intoned* is just the right word to use with this quote by this speaker?

picturesque. When they sink below a certain level a succinct paraphrase is the answer:

The senator said that "during this period of time, which covered six years, this subcommittee held a total of only six days of hearings."	The senator said the subcommittee held only six days of hearings in as many years.

The main distinction of the senatorial statement is 10 superfluous words.

Good quotes should summarize what's on a person's mind, crystallize an emotion or attitude, offer an individual perspective of some sort — preferably in a concise and interesting way.

Two examples, both from *The New York Times*. Here's a woman quoted in an account of life in Nicaragua:

"We can't make ends meet," said a 36-year-old waitress and mother of three who lives in the capital. "Everything's going up. We used to buy meat most days, but that's out of the question. We have to line up for hours for sugar and rice. And then we're told we can't have wage increases."

And this from a story about Northern Ireland's Maze prison, where IRA men were starving themselves to death:

"By the time they get in here, there's no more belligerence, no more fight," said an attendant in the one-story, 10-bed hospital. "They're really quite cooperative and polite at this final stage. They just sit there and quietly die."

A paraphrase would have been sinful.

When quotation marks, with their small subliminal drumroll, signal a human voice, the reader expects a pitch different from dryly factual recitation. Nothing but disappointment in the following story:

MIAMI — More than 6,300 exotic birds, from tiny finches to large parrots and macaws worth as much as $5,000 apiece, have been de-

stroyed at an import center because of an outbreak of Newcastle dis-
ease, a virus that kills domestic poultry, federal officials said.

"All the birds here were destroyed and we are in the process of
cleaning and disinfecting the area," said Connie Crunkelton, a
spokeswoman for the U.S. Department of Agriculture.

Miss Crunkelton said federal officials feared that infected birds
may have been shipped from Pet Farms Inc., the import company,
within the past 30 days.

"We have notified the animal health officials in the states" known
to have received shipments, she said. "They will go to the facility and
see if there are any infected birds. If so, they will have to be destroyed
and the owners will be reimbursed for their loss."

There were 123 species and subspecies among the 5,300 birds destroyed at Pet Farms, Miss Crunkelton said. The owner will be reimbursed for the loss, she said.

"We don't have a dollar estimate on the birds as of yet, but we expect one later," Miss Crunkelton said.

Putting such pedestrian, fact-sheet kind of information
into direct quotation is like trying to set the telephone di-
rectory to music. A few words of paraphrase could have dis-
patched the details.

The Uses of Quotes

Besides adding living voices to the script, quotes perform
certain standard functions. They are used to:

● Document and support third-person statements in
the lead and elsewhere.

● Set off controversial material, where the precise
wording can be an issue, as in legal contexts.

● Catch distinctions and nuances in important passages of speeches and convey some of the flavor of the
speaker's language.

● Highlight exchanges and testimony in trials, hear-
ings, meetings and other garrulous encounters.

Quotes should pull lustily on the oars to help move the
story along, as in this example:

SAN SALVADOR (AP) — Terrorists fired three anti-tank rocket grenades at the United States Embassy today, causing some damage but apparently no injuries, security forces reported.

They said the grenades were probably fired from a building about 60 yards away from the embassy compound.

"Something put a hole in one of our upper stories, but as far as we can tell nobody was hurt," said an embassy spokesman reached by telephone.

Another embassy employee said the damage was on the third floor, which houses the office of Ambassador Robert E. White, but the ambassador was not in the embassy at the time.

The third graf backs up the lead and adds a bit of fresh detail. Repetition is the great danger. Even robust quotes turn sickly as a reprise of something that's just been reported in third-person:

The chairman announced that the company would start the most ambitious engineering project in its history.

"We'll launch our most ambitious engineering project ever," he told applauding stockholders.

Following is an example of tiresome reiteration in the intro of a political campaign story. Quotes and paraphrase plod through four paragraphs around a single point already clear in the first:

SAN FRANCISCO — Republican vice presidential nominee George Bush accused Carter administration officials of distorting Ronald Reagan's positions to portray a president who might lead the nation into war.

In remarks prepared for delivery to the Commonwealth Club of San Francisco, Bush said the attack on his presidential running mate was "false and irresponsible."

Bush made the charge against unnamed "high-level spokesmen of the Carter administration" who, he said, "misrepresented Reagan's commitment to peace."

"Their objective is to portray Ronald Reagan as a man who, as president, might lead the country into war," Bush said. "It is a false and irresponsible distortion of Reagan's views as well as of his lifelong record as a citizen and public servant."

"False and irresponsible" appears twice after the same

thought is suggested by "distorted" in the lead. Misrepresenting Reagan's commitment to peace, furthermore, is the same as distorting his views to that effect. The whole business can be reported at half the length and without repetition by bringing the key quote into the lead:

> SAN FRANCISCO — Republican vice presidential nominee George Bush accused Carter administration officials of trying to portray Ronald Reagan "as a man who, as president, would lead the country into war."
>
> In remarks prepared for delivery at the Commonwealth Club of San Francisco today, Bush attributed "irresponsible distortion" to unnamed high-level spokesmen for the Carter administration. He said they "misrepresented Reagan's commitment to peace."

An Artist at Work

By way of contrast, consider the following political story, this one with a high gloss of craftsmanship. It's by AP's Walter Mears, a Pulitzer Prize laureate, who was covering the Reagan campaign. His account wraps up a hectic day's appearances, speeches, remarks, comments and barbs, with due attention both to substance and entertaining verbal byplay.

Talk being the essence of campaigning, more than one-third of the story (which will be condensed here) was in direct quotation. The quotes flow naturally from the context, without any need for cumbersome transitions and explanatory back-tracking.

Each quote is carefully set up with enough information immediately ahead to make it instantly intelligible. An important point. Note also the succinct summary of the complicated Reagan-Carter dispute over energy policy, enabling readers to follow Reagan's rhetorical thrusts.

The smooth interplay of full and partial quotes, paraphrase, description and background richly convey the sense and sound of that day's political road show.

ERIE, Pa. (AP) — Ronald Reagan accused President Carter on Thursday of making up figures to defend a flawed energy policy, and suggested "that's one of the reasons why he's found an excuse for not debating. . . ."

The Republican presidential nominee, disputing Carter's rebuttal to his criticism of the administration's energy program, produced what amounted to a long-distance campaign debate.

It started when Reagan charged Wednesday in Cleveland that administration policies discourage energy production. Carter, at the White House, countered that Reagan made the accusation without checking the facts. And Reagan retorted Thursday:

"Unfortunately, Mr. Carter's 'truth' again consists largely of misleading rhetoric and incomplete facts.

"You know, there are some people who look up the figures and some people who make up the figures," Reagan told a campaign crowd that filled the lawn of the Erie County Courthouse and stretched halfway along a tree-shaded block.

Earlier, in Buffalo, N.Y., Reagan told union men that he is a friend of organized labor. He said they cannot bargain for better wages or anything else "if Jimmy Carter keeps you out of a job." He said pickets who showed up chanting "We Want Carter" don't understand his own union record with the Screen Actors Guild.

In Erie, Reagan repeated his assertion that Carter policies "have discouraged the discovery and production of energy in this country."

Then he turned to a point-by-point rebuttal of Carter's energy statements.

Reagan said Carter "tried to boast about increased coal production," but the National Coal Association says 100 million tons of coal-producing capacity is idle and 22,000 coal miners are out of work.

"Now it's no surprise to me Mr. Carter is trying to distort his record on energy," Reagan said. "Like his economic and foreign policies, his energy policies have been so damaging to this country he doesn't want to talk about them."

Reagan said that without "the lucky bonanza of increased oil production from Alaska which Mr. Carter inherited," U.S. oil imports during the first half of 1980 would be 34 percent higher than in 1976.

"Mr. Carter says I spoke without checking the facts," Reagan said. "The truth is, it is Mr. Carter who didn't check the facts. . . .

"You don't suppose that that's one of the reasons why he's found an excuse for not debating, do you, that he wouldn't like a chance to compare these facts face to face," Reagan said.

Carter has refused an invitation to debate Reagan and independent John B. Anderson on Sept. 21. "He's using Mr. Anderson as an excuse," Reagan said. "Now I don't find Mr. Anderson much to be afraid of. But then, in the primaries, he found Teddy Kennedy too much for him to debate also."

After the speech, Reagan toured a General Electric plant. . . .

No Afterthoughts, Please

When a story is well organized, as that one was, quotes will fall effortlessly into place. When a story isn't, they seem like afterthoughts, usually requiring awkward explanatory tails:

> Anderson, winding up his campaigning in the Los Angeles area, conceded that the President might have a short-term political gain by refusing to appear on the same platform with the congressman. But in the long run, the Independent predicted, Carter would lose some support.
> "It's all politics," Anderson said *of Carter's position on the debate question.*

This is numbing prose all the way; the writer has Anderson refer to himself as *the congressman,* who in the next sentence mysteriously becomes *the Independent.* In any case, the amplification at the end of the second paragraph could have been avoided by putting the quote in its proper place:

> Anderson, winding up his campaigning in the Los Angeles area, conceded that the President might have a short-term political gain by refusing to appear on the same platform with him.
> "It's all politics," Anderson said. He predicted it would cost Carter support in the long run.

Pertinence May Decide

Newsworthy speeches, whether scintillating or not, require considerable direct quotation. Since you're usually working from a text, you can browse for quotes at some leisure. Here pertinence overrides color: It's advisable to give significant passages in the speaker's own words, even if they are fairly tedious.

This was not a problem in the following example, a happy meeting between a strong, expressive text and a writer, John Edlin, who knew how to make the most of it, from cutting the partial quote of the lead to the extended quotation in the last paragraph:

SALISBURY, Zimbabwe (AP) — Prime Minister Robert Mugabe said Thursday the black states of southern Africa must free themselves from foreign economic exploitation that has made them either "puppets or perpetual beggars."

Mugabe, opening the ministerial session of the Southern African Development Coordination Conference at a Salisbury hotel, accused unscrupulous foreign investors of maintaining a relentless grip on southern Africa's resources.

"We remain dominated economically by economic lords as we were politically dominated by political lords yesterday," said the prime minister of newly independent Zimbabwe, the former British colony of Rhodesia. "Economic domination is indeed a worse phenomenon than political domination."

Mugabe said "our resources are wasting away day by day as they get freighted to Paris, London and New York."

He said the nine nations taking part in the conference on "economic liberation" have recognized that they are "fragmented, grossly exploited, and subject to economic manipulation by outsiders."

The prime minister particularly criticized multinational corporations which he said arrange a "mouse's share for us and a lion's share for themselves." Black African nations, he said, are imprisoned by unfavorable trading conditions. They sell their raw material cheaply but have to pay "exorbitant" prices for imports.

"Thus we meet foul play in both cases," he said. "And whether we play at home or away, ours is perpetual defeat, theirs perpetual victory. Is it any wonder that we have been turned into either economic puppets or perpetual beggars?"

The reader has enough in Mugabe's own words to judge both substance and tone of his argument and catch a glint of his personality as well.

Help Wanted (Sometimes)

Quotes sometimes need a little internal stitching. A good parenthetic insert may be used to explain a technical word or to clarify a pronoun reference: *He said he had no idea why he (Smith) didn't show up for work with the others.*

But a little stage-whispering goes a long way. It's drowning out the quote here:

"I guess he (the driver) just hates hitchhikers. They (highway motorists) do it all the time. They swerve at you like they're trying to hit you. This is the first time one of us (referring to highway tramps in general) ever really got hit."

When a quote needs that much help, you're better off paraphrasing.

The ellipsis (. . .) indicates omitted matter. The trouble is that it calls attention to what is not rather than to what is. It's sometimes necessary, for example in quoting government reports or legal documents when sentences are excerpted from a coherent larger passage. But an ellipsis is seldom required in the ordinary run of conversational and interview quotes, which readers know to be excerpts anyway.

Clues and identification enabling readers to understand a quote normally should precede rather than follow it; the cryptic quote at the start of a paragraph is an annoyance.

That optimism assumed that passengers would return fairly quickly, airline executives say. But doubts about safety, along with a soft economy, have kept large numbers of passengers away, producing grim near-term prospects for several carriers.

"I don't agree with that," said Frank Borman, chairman of Eastern Airlines, about the view that the carriers would profit from the slowdown.

The reader is momentarily misled into believing that the disagreement refers to the grim near-term prospects.

The *Said of* Trap

Writers sometimes plunge into the *said of* mode to clarify something that's already clear from the context:

> While the players did not know that Michael was on the verge of being dismissed yesterday, they knew his job had been on the line at least once this season and, based on their experience, they knew that the team's principal owner often pressures and embarrasses his employees in a belief that it will improve their performance.
> "That may work in one facet of life but not in this one," Watson *said of* Steinbrenner's techniques.
> "Stick will be here," George Steinbrenner *said of* him that day last November.

Could it possibly have referred to anything or anybody else?

> Muskie devoted much of the news conference to the Iranian hostages.
> He cautioned that developments in Tehran had repeatedly disappointed the nation in the past.
> "We don't want to raise false hopes now," he *said of* the Iranian hostage situation.

He wasn't talking about his Aunt Nellie.

> "It's rare. We don't usually get that many large petitions," Richard Markse, a railroad spokesman, *said of* the 300 signatures Fields collected.

More clearly put:

> Fields collected 300 signatures. "It's rare," said Richard Markse, a railroad spokesman. "We don't usually get that many large petitions."

From a story about a dowser's trade:

> "I feel a little tingle and it starts moving," Austin *said of* his divining rod.

Clueing the reader in more effectively:

> Describing the workings of his divining rod, Austin said, "I feel a little tingle and it starts moving."

Haphazard Attribution

Make sure the reader always knows who's speaking, but don't overattribute in running quotations:

"I call that dead water. I can't find dead water in underground caverns." Austin calls moving water "love water" and says that is the only water he can find. "It's got to have some movement to it," *the dowser said.*

Don't drop attribution haphazardly into a quote where it will disrupt the flow of a sentence:

"The charge is not," the lawyer said, "warranted in the slightest degree."

"This is the second time," the angry senator said, "the agency has violated its own regulations."

Put the sinuous lawyer and the angry senator at the start or at the end of their sentences. When attribution goes within a sentence, it should fit smoothly between clauses or where a speaker might naturally pause:

"I thought I'd be free long before then," she said, "but it hasn't worked out that way."

Fragmentary Quotes

An indiscriminate rage to quote, or perhaps a sense of insecurity, traps writers into pointless fragmentary quotes, consisting of one or two unremarkable words used in their ordinary sense:

The mayor said a "key" element of his plan was the parking complex. He noted it had the support of "many citizens."

The critic called it a "wonderful" movie.

Had our critic called it "incandescent," however, quotation marks would be proper. The word is sufficiently unusual to rate the epaulets.

The quotation marks also are justified in cases like the following:

> When arrested, Smith said he was an "importer." (*To convey doubt.*)

> The president said Reagan was in no sense a "racist." (*To make clear that the president himself used this highly charged word.*)

> The Soviet news agency Tass said today that "criminal activities" had occurred in Kabul. (*In the West, it's Afghan resistance to the takeover.*)

Watch the Context

Next to getting the actual words right, the most important thing is to keep quotes in context. Failure usually arises from careless compression that makes a statement appear more emphatic than it is. A qualification may be dropped or buried, a speaker's elaboration of a point overlooked, or a remark intended as jocular reported deadpan.

It may be tiresome when a newsmaker surrounds his assertions with *ifs, buts* and *maybes,* but if he elects to crawl, the writer must not force him into a trot.

Special caution is indicated with the use of partial quotes in leads. Qualifications should either stay within the quote or follow immediately. Even if the full quote, with its amplified or softened meaning, appears later in the story, it's not enough; the reader may not get that far.

Consider the full statement on the left and the new version on the right:

"There may be occasions, crimes, when the death penalty appears justified. At least many people think so. I have sometimes leaned that way myself, but to my mind, large problems always remain."	A longtime opponent of capital punishment said today that on occasions "the death penalty appears justified." "I have sometimes leaned that way myself," he added, though "large problems always remain."

The partial quotes are accurate, but the meaning — the tentative tone — has been subtly altered.

Not so subtle is what befell Secretary of the Interior James Watt, who found himself sandbagged with a striking sentence that was widely quoted without the rest of the passage.

At a congressional hearing, Watt was asked if he believed that some resources should be conserved for future generations. His full reply:

> "Absolutely. That is the delicate balance the secretary of the interior must have to be steward for the natural resources for this generation as well as future generations. *I do not know how many future generations we can count on before the Lord returns.* Whatever it is, we have to manage with a skill to have the resources for future generations."

Perhaps an official sophisticated about the ways of the media should have scented peril in injecting religious musings into his testimony, but those who seized on the italicized sentence in isolation certainly conveyed a meaning different from that of the complete passage. It's something the conscientious newswriter will guard against.

You can also skewer a quote by converting a long, involved question into the subject's answer:

Reporter: *Do you feel the verdict was wrong, that it was a gross miscarriage of justice?*

A: *Well, yes.*

Copy: *He said "he felt that the verdict was wrong and a gross miscarriage of justice."*

Did he? Reporters shouldn't ask speechifying questions, but some will, especially at televised news conferences. You deal with it by clearly differentiating: *He said "yes" to a reporter's question whether he felt, etc.*

In the following passage, the practice is carried to absurdity:

> Eighty-seven percent of those surveyed in the national poll said "they feel personally, deeply involved with the fate of the hostages and are willing to wait as long as necessary to get the hostages back unharmed."

Must have been an interesting chorus. The quote, of course, refers to the survey question.

Never attribute a direct quote to more than one person, unless you've stumbled on a tribe that speaks in unison. The following appeared in a newspaper:

> Feminists hurled abuse as the men competed in a Bavarian park to become the fastest tree planter. "We don't accept the perpetuation of the masculine image," they yelled.

The *New Yorker* ran the item under the heading, "Yells We Doubt Ever Got Yelled."

Over-extended Attribution

Although indirect quotation offers more latitude, there are similar traps. Be sure not to attribute to the source wording and coloring obviously different from the source's own:

> WASHINGTON — The nation's unemployment rate shot up from 6.2 percent to 7 percent in April, the highest level in 2½ years *and a powerful sign that the inflation-wracked economy is now being squeezed by the vise of recession,* the government reported today.

All very true, no doubt, but that's not how the government's report put it.

In the following instance, the attribution is just over-extended:

> "It affects your whole life," said Wilson's pretty wife, Nancy, whose job as a court clerk helps to sustain them. "You're on edge. It's like a disease you're waiting to catch."
>
> The disease has reached epidemic proportions in the black community, which suffers from a jobless rate of 30 percent, says the Rev. Thomas Robinson, head of the Opportunity Industrialization Center.

The Reverend Robinson, however, didn't say anything about diseases and epidemics. A period after *community* and a new sentence would keep things straight.

A Band-aid May Help

We have stressed that direct quotes must faithfully reproduce what the speaker has said. There are times, however, when in an interview, minor grammatical slips could be corrected; hardly anyone is free of such mistakes in casual speech. The purpose is not to make anyone look good, but to make things easier for the reader.

For example, a story quoted Secretary of the Treasury Regan as saying: "Jim Baker knows more about politics than I'll ever know. But I think I know more about finances than *him.*" The writer could safely have made that *he*, or, better yet, stopped the quote at *finances.*

Note we are talking about mini-adjustments. Heroic intervention to straighten out gaping incoherencies is another matter. When a politican, say, replies to a question in a way that betrays monumental trouble in coming to grips with it, don't tighten and smooth quotes into a masterpiece of concise statement. Judgment, fairness and evenhandedness are the guides to navigating these shoals.

What about people who speak generally poor English, street language, use *ain't* and *that there's*? How far you go in using off-beat idiom depends on the purpose of the story. If it's to portray life in the Appalachian hollows, snippets of non-standard English, peculiar phrasing, the occasional double negative will add depth and flavor without offense.

But in most news stories, such speechways are simply irrelevant. You might call attention to a man's limp if he's just entered a track meet, but not if he's walking to the subway.

To illustrate from a story about a tavern shooting in Oregon:

No motive for the shooting was established.

"He didn't say nothing," said Brent Yagle, a patron of the popular nightspot frequented by people mostly in their 20s. "He just opened the door and started firing. I didn't think the shots were real until I saw people drop."

The tavern owner, John Helton, said, "I do hope he had some kind of reason and didn't do it just 'cause he was in the mood."

The double negative and bobtailed *because* merely contribute a whiff of condescension. Better to paraphrase the first: *The man said nothing, according to Brent Yagle . . .* And spelling out *because* would have violated no higher truth.

The following underscores the distinctions involved in this minor housebreaking. Saul Pett plumbed the mood of Asheville, N.C., in an election year. His intro centers on a series of quotes:

"Half this country keeps the other half going," says a bitter housewife in line at the checkout counter. Ahead of her is a man buying more meat than she can afford. He pays with food stamps.

"We can't do anything about those crazy Iranians holding our people," writes a rural editorialist, "but we can do something about taxes. We can control them."

"I'm relatively affluent, but will I be able to send my kids to college?" asks the executive director of what used to be a pillar of American optimism, the local Chamber of Commerce.

"The election?" ponders an old mountaineer. "I *ain't* heard it mentioned except on the TV."

The last quotee appears in the character of a mountaineer, an archtype, you might say, and the *ain't* is as natural as the plug of tobacco in a pitcher's cheek. No need to paraphrase.

Expletive Deleted

Profanity, vulgarity and obscenity present another kind of problem. Society has become vastly more permissive toward them in most forms of print, films and theaters. Newspapers, however, still avoid using such expressions — on grounds of taste in dealing with a very diversified audience, and also because blue language in a medium of information mostly distracts readers from the business at hand.

The limits of the acceptable vary from newspaper to newspaper. Each has its own well-defined policy (which doesn't preclude occasional soul-searching).

It's good advice — and AP policy — to avoid casual profanity and vulgarisms. Many swear words and expletives are so routine at certain levels of conversation in many groups that they're like other verbal fillers that can simply be dropped from a direct quote. When that seems awkward, paraphrase.

The practical test on admitting expletives is whether they are essential to the story. They seldom are. A celebrated exception was Jimmy Carter's unpresidential language referring to Sen. Edward Kennedy in promising to *"whip his ass."* Even so, some papers fig-leafed the noun with dashes or asterisks.

The mild profanity in the following example is also indispensable in giving the earthy flavor of a tough lady who had kept federal inspectors off her coal mine at gunpoint:

> When her cousin tried to fetch her she leveled a pistol at him and told him to get lost. A masher got fresh once while she was waiting tables and she scalded him with coffee. Her refusal of favors to another man included smashing his windshield with a tire iron. Don't cross Violet Smith.
>
> "Hell, kid, them feds have never scared me.
>
> "One time when I was running a little grocery in Durango, an Internal Revenue agent came in and said I haven't paid my taxes. I had. I flattened the S.O.B. with my fist and kicked his rear end out of the door."
>
> Violet Smith, incidentally, does not abbreviate S.O.B.

Paraphrase to the Rescue

A few final points on quotes:

• We're not in the business of protecting people from their own flapping tongues, but it's poor practice to make somebody look foolish in print when he has innocently misspoken himself:

> "What is lacking is not indifference and apathy," suggests Joseph Guinn, vice president of the association. "The general public just doesn't understand the educational value."

He meant that apathy and indifference were not the problem, and both he and the reader should have been rescued by paraphrase.

● Here you have the right way and the wrong way of using fragmentary quotes in one sentence:

> ATLANTA — A police officer testified today that he stopped Wayne B. Williams near a Chattahoochee River bridge because a "loud splash" made the officer "pretty suspicious."

The first phrase doesn't rate the quotation marks; the second does, as the precise description of his feelings.

● The more quotes resemble dialogue in form, the livelier they are. An exchange gives readers a special sense of participation. Here's an example from a routine news conference:

> Dick Moe, an aide to Vice President Mondale, told reporters: "I think both sides are in a position to go to the other and, depending on who prevails, seek their support in the general election."
> "And get it?" he was asked.
> "And get it."

In some stories, usually features, it's possible to trim superstructure for a similarly crisp effect. Compare the elaborate setups on the left with the version on the right:

When asked if she admired her mother's cooking, Miss Johnson replied, "It was fabulous." In response to a query about her own cooking skill, she conceded it was "not so hot."	What of her mother's cooking? "Fabulous." Her own? "Not so hot."

● Partial quotes should fit into the grammatical structure of the sentence.

The chairman emphasized that he "insists on equal pay for equal work."

Did he say, *"I insists?"* No. So move the opening quotation mark or paraphrase.

● Avoid double attribution:

The commissioner said he would move promptly against what he called "an outrageous situation."

Either *what he called* or the quotation marks, but not both.

● As in a primitive ritual, certain quotes recur automatically in similar news situations. People have many times read or heard those phrases and will mouth them when opportunity offers. By now these quotes have the appeal of bovine cud. But unless someone breaks the chain, they will continue until they become the last syllables of recorded time. Here are a few such prefabricated phrases that ought to be passed by:

"It's a great challenge." Starlet about her new role, executive about his new job, coach on taking over a team of ragged bums.

"I like people," in various nauseating configurations. Worth quoting if a mass murderer says it.

"It sounded like 10 (15, 100) freight trains." Applicable to all tornadoes.

"It sounded like an atom bomb going off." Any explosion. If he's actually heard an atom bomb going off, write about him.

COLOR: Dip Your Brush in Small Details

7

Elsewhere in this book we discuss how reporters need to develop a good ear to fit words together gracefully. To fit words together colorfully, they need to develop a good eye.

For color implies a way of *seeing* a story so you can *show* the reader. Adjectives and intensifiers have nothing to do with it — they are, in fact, great deceivers.

Why inform readers that something is dramatic or tragic? Give them the particulars, and they will supply their own adjectives.

What real image do you call up by describing a resort as *posh* or a military reservation as *sprawling*? What's distinctive about the *white, sandy* beach? Most beaches are. Or about the city that *is a city of many contrasts*? The same can be written about every city, and probably has been.

Color is a matter of detail — those details that make *this* story what it is, namely, different from any other stories in some precise circumstances. It works even in a report as routine as one on a city council hearing:

As the hearing droned on past midnight, half the audience had left. But the woman in the front row was still knitting away at her red sweater. In back, a middle-aged man, head down, was snoring gently. Councilman Smithers seemed to be counting the patches of peeling plaster on the walls, while Saunders rested his chin on the gavel. There was no further need of pounding.

Small, small details and a splash of real color in an unlikely setting. How many reporters would have gone to the trouble?

Here's a passage from a column by the late Red Smith, describing a morning at the race track:

> Through the fragrance of the wood fires burning under the elms in the stable area behind Saratoga's main track, wreaths of morning mist curled up to be burned away by slanting rays of sunshine. Hotwalkers led horses in lazy circles behind the barns, while their horses stood relishing the flow of cold water from garden hoses trained on their forelegs.
>
> Grooms swathed horses with soapy sponges and rubbed them dry. The rhythmic throbbing of hooves could be heard from the track itself, where the horses were working.

Here's a passage from another sports writer, describing a high moment in a World Series game:

> And attempting to overcome the Yankee lead was outfielder Clint Hurdle, tall, proud descendant of his Plains Indian forebears. But like tribesmen of the Old Indian wars, he faced a lethal sharpshooter equipped with a Winchester. Relief pitcher "Goose" Gossage would prove George Steinbrenner a box office wizard. In Boston, his speed blazed past the best of the Bosox. . . . He fired two strikes past a raging Hurdle who stood defiant at the plate . . . . And then a third swinging strike and one could hear war drums as Hurdle stared back at Gossage, unbelieving that he had bitten the dust.

The first is evocative and precise. The second, despite the hectic activity, the war drums, the Winchester, is tired.

Small, Specific Detail

For color, reporters cannot rely on phrases and fancy — or ready made — figures of speech. They rely on hard particulars. They must train themselves to spot those small, specific details that give intimate glimpses into the nature of the subject.

Jules Loh, in a profile of Herbert Hoover, noticed that among many items on the former president's desk was a tumbler containing a dozen well-sharpened pencils — a detail that most good reporters would pick up. But he also noticed that the erasers on all the pencils were worn down. That detail told more about the man than all the obvious ones: the color of his necktie, the shine on his shoes, the handkerchief in his breast pocket.

When Pulitzer Prize laureate Saul Pett wrote a story on the workings of the mind of Robert McNamara, he never once used the words *mind like a computer*. He didn't have to. He conveyed this idea by attention to detail during a dinner interview, describing McNamara as:

> . . . judiciously weighing the options of having a second drink or not, evaluating all the factors in selecting between fish or beef and, once having made up his mind, never looking back.

Sometimes it's difficult or inconvenient to plod after details, but that's where Joe Smith, the writer, relies on Joe Smith, the reporter. AP Newsfeatures writer Sid Moody discussed this in a postscript to a story he wrote about an ocean crossing on a square-rigged Norwegian sailing ship:

> You're looking for detail, verbs of description instead of adjectives or adverbs. Sure, the helmsman stands at the wheel like a Viking. But he also clamps his lips into a line to keep out the rain, narrows his eyes to gunslits against the wind, stares transfixed as a swami at the compass light. His knuckles are white from the cold and the strain of the helm. He sails on. The reader may have his own idea of what a Viking is, but you're out there in the wet to tell him what this particular Viking did on this particular ship in this particular storm, and if you can't give him specifics, you might as well go below and be warm and dry and eat goat yogurt.

Pseudo-Color Won't Work

No, grand generalizations and indistinct noun-adjective combinations don't add color to writing; particulars do. Here's an example of pseudo-color from a news story about a newly appointed immigration commissioner:

> Outside the state capitol he is said to be essentially mild-mannered. With his modishly styled hair, neat mustache and hornrimmed glasses, he could be taken for a professor from the nearby University of Texas.

On the basis of that description, so could half the male population. And note the ponderous qualifier before that daring characterization, mild-mannered. Pope John Paul II is mild-mannered, and so was Willie Sutton, the bank robber. Finally, what does a college professor look like? There are college professors who could be taken for plumbers, undertakers, corporation chairmen, engineers and confidence men.

This kind of mush just amounts to a string of words, adding up to a cliché portrayal that you've read before in a thousand inconsequential contexts.

Contrast this terse sentence in an AP story describing a craftsman who reproduces Shaker furniture:

> Charles Caffal is a 43-year-old artisan, built along the lines he admires most. He is as lean as a clothespin — a Shaker invention — and his only ornamentation is a full, reddish beard.

This is a rich image in a few words, and a long way from the essentially mild-mannered, bespectacled gent who could be taken for your typical college professor.

So is this line, from a *New York Times* story:

> On hills that are normally green at this time, there's nothing but a sere, parched, dun-colored stubble.

Many writers have made a perfunctory bow to color with "drought-stricken hills." The quoted sentence is intensely visual. And that *sere*? A difficult word, no doubt, for many readers, but the sense of the passage is not impaired for the ignorant, while the knowing might take pleasure in the echo from Shakespeare's "sere and yellow leaf."

Not every story lends itself to color. A presidential announcement, a report on rising interest rates, various government actions — not much chance for visual writing there.

But one suspects the writer of the following passage could have done better than toss in two pallid adjectives as perfunctory tints:

> Secretary of Defense Caspar Weinberger began his toast in the *ornate, formal* banquet hall of the Swedish foreign ministry.

For all the picture that gives, Weinberger might have started his toast in a packing crate. The reporter presumably had seen the place. What does *ornate* evoke? Cupids grinning from a frescoed ceiling? Curlicued pillars and fretwork? We don't see. And what does *formal* show you? Do these little labels pasted across *banquet hall* really perform any function? It's doubtful. When you want to describe, do it with precise detail. Otherwise, don't waste space.

Don't Overdo It

Flatness is the greater problem in news writing than excessive color, but color can be overdone. We have all suffered through crime stories where reporters ghoulishly dwelt on pools of blood and regaled us with the precise degree of decomposition of a body dead for nine weeks.

A scuffle between two drunks, however picturesque, at a political gathering doesn't rate a burst of description high in a report of a presidential candidate's campaign speech. Like so much else in this intricate business, color requires a sense of balance and proportion, impossible to define, and every colorful detail must pass the test of relevance.

The writer, having trained his eye to spot particulars with the intensity of a devout bird watcher, must come to the typewriter with a notebook crammed with them. And then have the discipline to use only those details that tell something about the subject. Details painstakingly collected are not easy to discard. The writer is often tempted to use them because he has them. Which may be why, in countless celebrity interviews, we're told that Miss Sexuality dispensed her bon mots over a tomato and watercress salad. (Mention the menu if it's filleted rattlesnake.)

When Color Works

Let us conclude the dissertation on color with three examples where, integral to each story, color works exactly right.

The first is from a story that dealt with a controversy about convict road crews. After outlining the issues and describing the work, writer Andrew Petkofsky of the *Richmond News leader* took his readers to the scene:

> The crew had started at the Henrico County line about a month before and worked steadily through some of the summer's hottest days.
> This day was cool and lovely, however, and the prisoners in blue work clothes and orange hard hats had plenty of time to gripe to a reporter as they hefted shovels, rakes and brooms. The uniformed young man standing guard with a 12-gauge shotgun listened impassively. He had heard it all before.

Note the precision of visual detail.

Example 2, from *The New York Times*, is equally vivid and concrete in another, more somber prison setting. It deals with a trial in Iran, and by the time readers reach the passage, they know the defendants will be shot.

> The two men, looking haggard in their stubble and rumpled clothes, are marched out of their two tiny rooms, around a small foun-

tain ringed by bright, yellow marigolds and into a bare room covered with revolutionary slogans and pictures of Ayatollah Khomeini.

The men sit in straight-backed wooden chairs, their guards stand a few feet away, pointing guns at them. The visitors take seats nearby. The prisoners squint, trying to adjust their eyes to bright light on this very sunny and pleasant day.

Third, consider this brushwork of vivid detail in a story by James A. Bacon in the *Roanoke* (Va.) *Times & World-News*, about a millionaire down on his luck:

Millions of dollars in debt, abandoned by friends and kin, Elkins was planning his comeback. A kitchen table, littered with dirty dishes and pizza crust, was his desk. An antiquated telephone dialed by the motel switchboard operator was his link to the outside world.

Five years earlier, "Covey" Elkins had been the most dazzling success story in the Virginia coal fields. . . .

Now the remnants of his empire are locked up in bankruptcy court. Gone is the mansion with its four-car garage, sauna and indoor swimming pool. Gone are the Lincoln Continentals, the helicopter, the fine clothes. And gone are the false friends and flatterers.

On an ice-bound winter afternoon, Elkins worked in the gloom of his motel room, tying up the phone for hours, trying to drum up credit, old coal equipment, overlooked coal leases — anything that could put him back in business.

Color is a way of seeing a story. On behalf of reporters who prefer to operate on sonar, like bats, we can only intone the Old Testament verse: "Lord, I pray thee open his eyes that he may see."

PSEUDO-COLOR: Cliches and Other Trespasses

8

We now pass from living color into the nether world of clichés, misshapen figures of speech and strained comparisons. These, too, spring from the laudable impulse to brighten copy, but the tools are shoddy and so are the results.

Clichés by definition are threadbare phrases that good writers try to avoid. George Orwell, a purist in style, advised long ago: "Never use a metaphor, a simile, or a figure of speech that you are used to seeing in print."

The general idea is sound, but the prohibition too sweeping. No writer can do entirely without the large stock of familiar expressions that includes hard-working idiom, phrases somewhere between idiom and cliché (off base, snowed under) and clichés unalloyed.

The late Eric Partridge, who heroically compiled a *Dictionary of Clichés,* conceded that what constitutes a cliché is partly a matter of opinion. Set a brace of editors to hunting down clichés in the same story and some of their trophies will be different; one may gag at a phrase that doesn't ruffle the other.

The way in which you use a tired expression also bears on its cliché status. Sir Ernest Gowers, another accomplished word man, says it depends on whether clichés "are used unthinkingly as reach-me-downs or chosen as the best means of saying what a writer has to say."

Furthermore, not all clichés are obnoxious to the same degree. Some are so abysmal that no self-respecting writer will touch them in any context: *Selling like hotcakes, breath of fresh air, last but not least, shun like the plague, leave no stone unturned* are among the pariahs. (A selected list of other mangy expressions appears at the end of this section.)

But in many cases, no summary beheading is necessary. *Sour grapes, swing of the pendulum,* and *white elephant,* for example, are greatly worn. Yet each wraps up a rather complicated situation succinctly, and if your alternative proves labored and verbose, you're better advised to stick to the cliché.

Clichés at Arm's Length

Here are a few suggestions on dealing with clichés — at proper arm's length (cliché? idiom?) but without hysteria:

1. Don't worry about an occasional cliché, but start stringing a few together and your story wilts. With each additional cliché in a passage, the staleness increases exponentially. That's what happened in the following political story:

> 1st graf: They're *throwing out the rule book* in Nassau County.
> 3rd graf: Caso is *not taking it lying down.*
> 7th graf: Some say Margiotta has not enforced the peace because 1) he is *licking elective wounds,* 2) he is *gun-shy* from federal investigations of several Republicans and wants to *shed his boss image* for a *low profile,* or 3) he believes it's the right thing to do.

> 10th graf: In the spring, he announced his availability, widely re-
> garded as a move to force Caso's maneuvers *out of the
> closet.*

No story can weather that many banalities. The last figure, incidentally, is not only a cliché, but a mangled one:
politicians might maneuver in a smoke-filled room, but
hardly in a closet.

2. A cliché is acceptable when it serves your meaning precisely: *The city for years has tried to rid itself of these white
elephants.* Never use a cliché as decoration or for emphasis;
it has lost all power and glitter: *The rumor swept the town
like wildfire.*

3. Don't use a cliché as a facetious way to inflate a simple
idea: *By the end of the year, the long arm of the law had
caught up with him. (The law had caught up with him.)*

4. When you must use a cliché, get it right. Don't *throw
out the baby with the dishwater (bathwater).* Don't say, as
a senator recently did, that *we're all working like banshees.* (Banshees *wail.*) Or make it, as a government secretary commenting on her boss's absence did, *when the wolf
is away, the mice will play.* (Although that might have
been a Freudian slip.)

5. It's impossible to freshen a cliché, so let it slide past
quietly without tinkering with it. *They put the fancy cart
before the old horse* merely underscores the poverty of the
phrase.

6. Don't put clichés in quotation marks or apologize for
them coyly with an *as the old cliché has it.* Inviting the
reader to hold his nose just calls attention to the odor.

7. Don't dress up your copy with Great Quotations that have been ground into commonplaces: *East is East and West is West and never the twain shall meet* (Kipling); *a rose by any other name . . . the slings and arrows . . . to be or not to be,* (Shakespeare); *A rose is a rose is a rose,* (Gertrude Stein). I hope to see one income tax deadline pass without a story reminding us that April is the *cruelest month* (T.S. Eliot). These and a hundred more, splendid in their original setting, have become debased currency by overborrowing.

8. If there is one way to squeeze juice from a cliché, it's by twisting it to yield a new and surprising meaning: *Bedfellows make strange politics.*

Sports Page Pariahs

Nowhere do clichés flourish more luxuriantly than on sports pages. It doesn't have to be this way, as good sports writers prove every day. But the weaklings succumb in droves to the handy platitude. There may be no excuses for it, but there's an explanation.

The subject matter, for one thing, is pretty much the same. Stanley Walker, one of the great newspapermen of any year, summed up one part of the problem nearly 50 years ago in his book *City Editor.*

"Almost every murder, suicide, shipwreck and train collision is cut on a different pattern, and the reporter does not have to seek outlandish substitutes for common terms. One baseball game, however, is pretty much the same as any other. The few standard verbs and nouns used in writing of baseball, football and boxing become tiresome."

In short, as the event loses flavor, some reporters tend to overseason their prose; plain words like *defeat, win, score* seem wan and are swept away in a blaze of synonyms. The writer reaches for baubles, instead of relying on eyes, ears and insight, and unfortunately the baubles are the common property of the tribe. (Political writers slogging through a long, repetitive campaign face similar temptations. In fact, sports clichés are freely imported into politics: You read of the frontrunner in a crowded field stumbling in a crucial primary while a dark horse is closing so fast that the convention will go right down to the wire.)

Second, some writers still treat sports as a mystical saga of superheroes, untainted by ordinary grit and grime of human endeavor. That approach doesn't foster understatement. (Great sports writers often have a soft spot for the more marginal athletes, who make it to the major leagues — barely — on effort and determination rather than an abundance of natural ability.)

Finally, there is the linguistic cannibalism in the closely knit world of sports, where writers, editors, coaches, athletic directors, players and publicists keep steady company and recklessly borrow from the sports pages and each other. As Walker said, "Some of these words and phrases were pithy and effective. The trouble was that when one writer hit upon a good phrase the others took it up and used it until it became threadbare." The chewing of communal cud still produces a stream of new clichés every week without abandoning the old.

A crescendo builds with the fatuous questions and prefabricated answers at recurrent rituals: the locker room quotes, the pre-game and post-game meditations of coaches, the profound speculations of managers about World Series prospects ("We'll just have to score more runs than they do").

A while ago Don Duncan, managing editor of the *Tacoma* (Wash.) *News Tribune,* took a deep breath and surveyed the sports cliché scene in a report for The Associated Press Managing Editors Association. He wrote:

Today's clichés wear the false mustaches and sunglasses of pop-psych, pseudo-science, the Kinsey report, old war stories and the medical journals.

Verbatim quotes from Sonny Superstar and Coach Win Handily enrich our native tongue and Logic I: "If we could have scored more, we would have won."

It was, our video display terminal-stained wretches tell us, "very physical out there, a real donnybrook, a Pier Six brawl."

Then the obligatory, "You've gotta give credit."

To whom? Why, the dee-fense, those who came to play, those who gave a 110 percent effort.

That's why the team didn't have to play catchup all afternoon.

Today's clichés are armor-clad and macho. The team penetrates, the deeper the better. The men up front stick, blitz and sack. The men in the trenches, the stop troops, dig in for a last-ditch stand. The rifle-armed field general succeeds because his team is quicker off the ball.

But first the team must establish the running game, so vital to ball control. It must earn respect up the middle. Only then will the game plan work, will it generate momentum.

Coach Handily prowls or stalks the sidelines, secure in the knowledge that he has recruited the best athletes available. He ignores the polls. He plays them one game at a time, absolutely refusing to show up in the wrong stadium on Saturday.

Coach Handily has no trouble getting his team up for the game because he respects the opposition, although (chuckle) they pull their pants on one leg at a time, the same as we do.

This respect — despite media belief that a laugher, a breather, even a romp is in the offing — stems from Handily's certainty that the other team is a lot better than its record (1-10). He knows the opposition will show up for the game, and that it can do a lot to hurt you (kneeing, tripping, grabbing the face mask and other cheap shots).

Fortunately, Coach Handily has a sophomore sensation (the logical development of last year's frosh phenom), a wide receiver, a veteran quarterback who can do a lot of things out there, and a promising kid at running back, pure poetry in motion, who is just possibly the best since Gayle Sayers.

Coach Handily's boys show their character in the stolid acceptance of penalties for holding and roughing the kicker (who pulled a Barrymore out there) and you have a contender, right in the thick of things, having a lot to say about who wins it.

Coach Handily's latest victim can hold up his head, being one of the class guys in the game today. His team always shows up, ready to go for broke, and is strong on the fundamentals.

"We were beaten by a fine football team," he says, "to which you gotta give a lot of credit. I guess they wanted it more than we did. But if we had executed, if we'd been more opportunistic, if we had followed the game plan and had been able to establish the running game, you gotta believe it would have been a lot closer.

"I'd also like to look at the game film, to check out some questionable calls by the referees near the end when we had some momentum going."

Writers are condemned to the cliché treadmill not by their subject matter, but by mental indolence. Red Smith wrote sports for nearly half a century until his death in 1982, but in his latter years you'd find fewer clichés in his copy than there are snakes in Ireland. "I have tried to become simpler, straighter, and more pure in my language," he once said. "I look at some of the stuff I wrote in the past and I say, 'Gee, I should have cooled it a little more.' "

The writer who finds himself drifting toward the hotter latitudes, not to say the cliché doldrums, should cool it a little more. Fifty years ago, Walker laid it out:

> The sports reading public today is remarkably well informed. It cannot be tickled by mere extravagance of writing. A lazy and incompetent writer finds it increasingly difficult to get by with a sloppy story, spun on a thread of artificial conceits. The demand is that he give his readers the facts, and give them straight. When crowds of 75,000 and more attend baseball and football games, and boxing matches, while millions more are listening on the radio, the sports writer should realize that he has an immense, well-informed audience that does not like to be fooled or short-changed.

And that was long before television increased the audience that could not only hear, but see for itself.

The Overreachers

Many clichés are metaphors and similes that have been worked to death but refused decent burial. Expert writers fluently devise their own, which helps make their language concrete and "pictureable." But there are perils, too, in groping for novelties, and tyros tend to overreach themselves. Figures of speech are slippery characters, valuable when they're on target, distracting when they misfire.

The apt figure of speech has remarkable power; an example is Saul Pett's phrase that New York's baldish mayor Ed Koch "blushed like a kosher pumpkin," and, in a different vein, Jules Loh's metaphor in describing the arrival of a white whooping crane in a flight of drab sand cranes: "As the formation winged past the curtain of a mountain, the whooper appeared as a single glistening pearl in a pale gray strand."

Splendid images. Try for such phrases, but don't try too hard; a strained figure of speech is usually ludicrous, dismal, or both.

In fact, when you're aglow with satisfaction over a newly hatched, unusual figure, give it a clinical second look. Such caution would have saved some embarrassment in the following newspaper examples:

> Interest rates are sprouting fresh skids today.

In a financial hot house?

> His eyebrows furrowed in a tempestuous stare.

Most people stare, non-tempestuously, with their eyes.

> Frustration, skepticism and humor juggled for the upper hand yesterday for those whose international odysseys were to have begun at the TWA terminal.

Quite a little carnival, but frustration, skepticism and humor are abstractions that don't juggle, and even jugglers don't juggle for the upper hand. The writer may have meant *jostle,* but that wouldn't help much, either.

Metaphors: Mixed and Protracted

Mixed metaphors are common misdemeanors:

> While the controversy is the latest storm to engulf him, it is the latest chapter in a long series of tangled events.

These are clichés, but a storm doesn't turn into a chapter.

A dead metaphor is sometimes brought to unseemly life by an active one:

> It was a rooted idea and it ran away with them.

Not unless you uproot it first.

> President Ford arrived in Medford, Ore., this morning as he continued his drive to throw sand into the motor of the Reagan juggernaut.

A juggernaut was a large wagon, drawn by beasts or men, and containing an idol of Krishna. (Followers threw themselves under the wheels to be crushed.) Hard to envision with motors and not applicable to the Reagan campaign.

> His neighborhood, nestled east of Grand Concourse and south of Fordham Road, while remaining a *womb* of friends, family and fellow Italian-Americans, has suffered from police layoffs, an increase in burglaries, and the destruction or abandonment of apartment buildings.

A womb generally doesn't nestle, though something is said to nestle in a womb. Worse, we're dealing with a giant and hyperactive womb.

Metaphors are sprinters, not long-distance runners. Know when to let go:

> Smith, an avid sailor, has been at the helm of his company five years, and during that time has steered it past many shoals.
> The worst squall he faced was a bitter proxy fight, but he weathered it and the seas have been calm since.
> In fact, the only one who makes waves now is Smith himself.

By the third paragraph, the reader needs a life preserver. Here's another protracted metaphor that should have been tackled before reaching the third graf:

CHARLOTTESVILLE, Va. — For the University of Virginia's enthusiastic but inexperienced offensive linemen, the first weeks of the college football season will represent trial by fire.

Will the searing heat of pressurized competition vaporize their pride and melt their competitive instincts, the way it did with their predecessors?

Or will it instead transform them into a strong, resilient alloy? Their coaches and teammates are anxiously awaiting an answer — for the success or failure of the offensive line will likely determine whether the Cavaliers' season glows brightly or soon flickers into unfulfilled darkness.

The Personification Peril

Personification, with allegory, was the literary rage in the 18th century, but it goes against the modern grain and today is the feeblest of metaphorical devices. Language itself, of course, personifies: We say that luck smiles, fate frowns, and the like. But this is unobtrusive. Not so when we trot out Old Man Winter, Father Time, Mother Nature and endow them with human traits.

Destiny's finger was about to tickle this man.
Winter thrust his icy fist into the nation's mid-section today.
He was riding high until Dame Fortune turned a cold shoulder.
The mercury struggled all day to climb above zero.

Frankly, my dear, the mercury doesn't give a damn.

Writing like this was on the wane when the weather service gave it fresh impetus with its disastrous decision to christen hurricanes. Some writers have found the temptation irresistible. Here's a milder example of what's done to our frolicsome tempests:

The petticoats of hurricane Belle sashayed through New Jersey toward a landfall on Long Island today, buckling a four-block section of Atlantic City's famed boardwalk. . .

Actually, if anyone sashayed it was Belle rather than her boardwalk-buckling petticoats, but it doesn't really matter.

Other Poisonous Mixtures

We've been considering verbal mishaps that shouldn't happen, but which carry no grievous consequences. It's different when, in chasing too hard after a clever, cute or poetic expression, a writer comes up with an incongruous analogy. Don't mix the important with the trivial, the serious with the silly. The brew can explode. Following are three examples where the results proved at best tasteless and at worst offensive:

BALTIMORE — The smoke has cleared from the Vatican's Sistine chapel, but the fire still smolders in the locker room of the troubled Baltimore Colts.

Equating a papal election with the intramural squabbles of a football team may be an original thought, but one that should have been still-born.

Then again, trying to find people who quit smoking for the day in the tobacco company's headquarters ranked right up there with soliciting for a birth control clinic in the Vatican.

An editor commenting on this passage in the paper's in-house bulletin said: "Hot stuff, maybe, for *Saturday Night Live,* but for our purposes it ranks right down there with Earl Butz's joke about the pope and birth control. Humor in news and feature stories has its limits. Being gratuitously clever and flippant about religious tenets exceeds those limits."

SEATTLE — Seattle Mariners designated hitter Richie Zisk has imposed a news blackout that would make Anwar Sadat proud. But unlike the Egyptian president who recently expelled a TV newsman from his country for what he considered inaccurate reporting, Zisk, the American League's leading hitter, has simply declined to comment on current events.

The irrelevance is staggering, the moral obvious. Don't reach. Keep your critical faculties awake. Does this parallel make sense? Is that comparison far-fetched? That humorous sally offensive? The metaphor mixed? The simile comparing apples with oranges? Is it perhaps just a decorative cliché?

When in doubt, strike it out. Even apt figures of speech should be used sparingly; too many create a filigree that's out of place in the simple, direct style. As Strunk and White note in *Elements of Style*, similes coming in rapid fire weary readers by asking them to compare everything with something else.

Words to Swear At

These clichés are among the dreariest in captivity, in one editor's opinion anyway. The list is not exhaustive. You may not find your favorite here;

armed to the teeth	burning issue
banker's hours	bury the hatchet
battle royal	calm before the storm
beat a hasty retreat	cherished belief
beauty and the beast	clear the decks
bewildering variety	club-wielding police
beyond the shadow of a doubt	colorful scene
bite the dust	conspicuous by its absence
blazing inferno	coveted award
blessed event	crack troops
blessing in disguise	curvaceous blonde
blissful ignorance	dramatic new move
bull in a china shop	dread disease
burn one's bridges	dream come true
burn the midnight oil	drop in the bucket

fame and fortune
feast or famine
fickle fortune
gentle hint
glaring omission
glutton for punishment
gory details
grief-stricken
grim reaper
hand in glove
hammer out (an agreement)
happy couple
hook, line and sinker
head over heels in love
heart of gold
heavily armed troops
iron out (problems)
intensive investigation
lady luck
lash out
last-ditch stand
leave no stone unturned
leaps and bounds
light at the end of the tunnel
lightning speed
limp into port
lock, stock and barrel
long arm of coincidence (the law)
man in the street
marvels of science
matrimonial bliss (knot)
meager pension
miraculous escape
mother nature
move into high gear
never a dull moment
old man winter
paint a grim picture
pay the supreme penalty
picture of health
pillar of (the church, society)

pinpoint the cause
police dragnet
pool of blood
posh resort
powder keg
pre-dawn darkness
prestigious law firm
proud heritage
proud parents
pursuit of excellence
radiant bride
red faces, red-faced
reins of government
rushed to the scene
scantily clad
scintilla of evidence
scurried to shelter
selling like hotcakes
spearheading the campaign
spirited debate
spotlessly clean
sprawling base, facility
spreading like wildfire
steaming jungle
stick out like a sore thumb
stranger than fiction
storm of protest
supreme sacrifice
surprise move
sweep under the rug
sweet harmony
sweetness and light
tempest in a teapot
tender mercies
terror-stricken
tip of the iceberg
tower of strength
trail of death and destruction
true colors
vanish in thin air
walking encyclopedia

wealth of information
whirlwind campaign

wouldn't touch with a 10-foot pole
last but not least

Doubleheaders

Lawyers love paired words with related meanings, like null and void, part and parcel, aid and abet, sum and substance, irrelevant and immaterial. They're kissing cousins of redundancies.

Leave such sing-song pleasures to the barristers. When a doubleheader comes to you unbidden, as it usually does, pause to consider if one word won't say it all:

beck and call
betwixt and between
bits and pieces
blunt and brutal
bound and determined
clear and simple
confused and bewildered
disgraced and dishonored
each and every
fair and just

few and far between
nervous and distraught
nook and cranny
pick and choose
ready and willing
right and proper
safe and sound
shy and withdrawn
smooth and silky
various and sundry

FEATURES: A View From the Poets' Corner

9

The hard news story marches briskly through the whats, whens, wheres, looking neither right nor left, packing in enough details to give readers a clear picture.

In features, the immediacy of the event is secondary. The plain ladder of descending news values is replaced by human interest, mood, atmosphere, emotion, irony, humor. Features aim to give readers pleasure and entertainment along with (and, on the fluffier side, sometimes in lieu of) information.

The range of features encompasses the gourmet column and Orphaned Dog of the Week as well as news enterprise of major significance. The more compelling features supplement the straight news content in timely and topical ways: they illuminate events, offer perspective, explanation and interpretation, record trends, tell people about people.

Because features are less shackled to the moment than hard news stories, writers usually have more time. Proper use of that time takes a special discipline. Some writers, unfortunately, use it to lard their copy with clusters of adjectives, purple passages and other decorative devices. If you feel the decorative impulse coming on, lie down until it goes away. Strong feature writing is simple, clear, orderly, free of labored mannerisms and tricks that call attention to the writing itself rather than the substance.

First, the Beginning

Most hard news stories follow a basic pattern. By comparison, the feature floats free. The writer has the choice of many approaches. This offers splendid opportunities to the skilled and imaginative, but it also holds traps for the unwary, particularly in the first several paragraphs, the intro.

There's never any doubt about the point of a straight news story; the lead tells you. In features, that point may be postponed. You don't have to play it out explicitly, in the first graf or two. But readers need to know soon what the story is all about, and why they should go on reading. Bury this crucial point too far beneath anecdote, description and atmospherics, and you'll exasperate readers rather than intrigue them. This is what happened in the following story:

> Come right in. Dinner will be ready in just a minute. Susie is making dinner tonight. You can hear her in the kitchen, talking to Connie Karli, who is in charge here.
> That's Connie's voice, telling Susie to make sure that none of the eggshells get into the bowl. Tonight, it's scrambled eggs, sausage and salad. It's slow going, with Connie steadily supervising.
> "You have to be careful with the shells," Connie says.
> "Why, Connie?" Susie asks, scrupulously scooping out eggshells with a fork. "Why do you have to be careful with the shells?"
> Susie is very cautious when she cooks; she takes great delight in serving a good meal, when it's over, but what she likes best is setting the table. Susie, who is 35, with dark hair and delicate skin, never cooked when she lived at home with her parents, but now she takes her turn making dinner.
> Since everyone moved in at 366 Highland Ave. the only major

renovations have been in the kitchen, which is now filled with new appliances. . .

The story continues for another long paragraph before readers are told they're visiting a home for the mentally retarded. Maybe some guessed, but more were probably wondering when the writer would get to the point.

Following are intros from two installments of a series on national parks. Both set the scene descriptively, but one rambles under a cloud of adjectives and generalities while the other goes straight to the heart of the story:

HATTERAS, N.C. — The narrow road that threads its way northward along Hatteras Island from Hatteras Inlet to the village of Nags Head has been called one of America's most scenic drives.

To the east, white-capped waves roll in from what early mariners knew as "The Graveyard of the Atlantic." Pamlico Sound, dotted with scores of fishing boats, sparkles to the west. Flocks of wild ducks and long-legged exotic birds perch on the high dunes along the road to Cape Hatteras National Seashore and Pea Island Wildlife Refuge.

In the winter, the Outer Banks region is isolated except for the hardy native fishermen. Tourists don't venture onto the storm-swept islands until the summer warms up the 75 miles of beaches and the dozens of motels and restaurants open for the season.

Readers must plod through two more paragraphs of this travel-brochure prose until they are told that the "scenic and historic" Outer Banks, like other barrier islands, are threatened by erosion, the sea and the carelessness of man.

Equally unfortunate, the writer doesn't offer a single fresh, personal observation of the wild beauties of the place but falls back on clustered adjectives: *scenic, historic, white-capped, storm-swept, hardy, exotic,* words trotted out automatically for such occasions.

Here's the second intro from the series, which gets swiftly and effectively to the point:

WASHINGTON — Chunks of ceiling plaster are strewn on the floor. When it rains, water stands three inches deep. Toadstools grow in one corner.

Welcome to Union Station, reborn by act of Congress 13 years ago as the National Visitors Center.

Following is a more leisurely anecdotal approach, from *The Wall Street Journal,* but this intro, too, leads straight to the subject:

LONDON — A year before he was overwhelmingly voted out of office as prime minister of Jamaica, Michael Manley gave a testimonial to his alma mater.

"The London School of Economics," he wrote, "had a profound influence on my early development. I find to this day that some of the habits of thought and analysis which I acquired at LSE are useful, some 30 years later."

Mr. Manley, an ardent Socialist, was widely blamed for the collapse of his country's economy. The London School of Economics, founded by the Fabians, is just as widely blamed for educating people like Mr. Manley in the ideals of British Socialism — its own invention — and sending them off to make a mess of the Third World.

At the end of the third (seductive) graf, the reader is firmly on course — and hooked. His interest is whetted. That is all a good feature intro need do. The significant elements of the story can be left for later. Here are the next two grafs, building toward a nice surprise:

With a reputation like that, it may seem fitting that the LSE is finally getting its financial comeuppance. It is suffering more than almost any other university in Britain as Margaret Thatcher's monetarist government hacks away at the supposed excesses of higher education in the welfare state. There is, however, an anomaly in this. British monetarism, it seems, is an LSE invention as well.

Much as Michael Manley's reputation may have been deserved, the LSE's is not. "It's one of the most bewildering things about being at LSE," says Ralf Dahrendorf, the German scholar and politician who became its director in 1974.

The school, renowned as a Socialist breeding ground, actually harbors what may be the most right-wing department of government in the West.

The last two paragraphs are important, indeed the "hard" substance of the story, but nothing was lost working up to them slowly. The writer could, of course, have started the piece like this:

> LONDON — The London School of Economics, reputed to be a propagator of Socialist ideas through its alumni in the Third World, actually harbors what may be the most right-wing department of government in the West.

That would seem acceptable as far as it goes, but flat and dry in comparison with the anecdotal, story-telling method the writer chose. This, of course, is the special appeal of the feature story.

The Interest Is *Human*

One problem with the dehydrated lead is that it is general. Moving from the general to the particular is seldom as effective in feature writing as the other way around. A broad-brush opener tends to be duller, unless the writer is unusually lucky or adroit. Whenever possible, raise the curtain on a human actor and human action, not a juiceless stage setting.

If, for example, you start a report on the effects of the Cuban influx on Miami with an "overview" of the emigres' influence on the city's economy, culture and politics, you're likely to wind up with an abstract catalogue that lacks human interest.

If, on the other hand, you start with an anecdote about an individual or family whose experience exemplifies one or more of these phenomena, the readers are instantly caught up in somebody's life. They'll follow that with greater interest than a parade of Issues and Problems.

Good feature writers capitalize on this and bring it off even where a particularized, human-interest focus seems hard to devise. Following is the beginning of a story by Saul Pett on the federal bureaucracy, an 8,500-word blockbuster that dealt with the size, pervasiveness and complexity of the government, how it got that way and with what mixed results — a story done well enough to win a Pulitzer Prize for Pett.

Technically, it is a masterful intro, piquing the reader's interest at every turn by foreshadowing with specifics all the main elements of a singularly complicated story.

WASHINGTON (AP) — We begin with the sentiments of two Americans two centuries apart but joined in a symmetry of indignation.

One said this: "He has erected a multitude of offices and sent hither swarms of officers to harass our people, and eat out their substance."

The other said this: "The government drives me nuts. The forms are so complicated I have to call my accountant at $35 an hour and my lawyer at $125 an hour just to get a translation."

The latter opinion belongs to Roger Gregory, a carpenter and small contractor from Sandy Springs, Md., a man of otherwise genial disposition.

The first statement was made by Thomas Jefferson, in the Declaration of Independence, in the bill of particulars against the king of England that launched the American Revolution.

It is one of the ironies of history that a nation born out of a deep revulsion for large, overbearing government is now itself complaining, from sea to shining sea, about large, overbearing government.

Somewhere between Thomas Jefferson and Roger Gregory, something went awry with our American growth hormone. And now in our 40th presidency, Ronald Reagan is trying to saddle and tame a brontosaurus of unimaginable size, ubiquity and complexity.

In designing a government, James Madison said, "the great difficulty is this: You must first control the governed and, in the next place, oblige it to govern itself." Has it?

Several things are noteworthy about this intro. With 8,200 words still to follow, the first three grafs, with the use of particulars, set the reader on a firm course. And when he moves from the particular to the general, the irony of the nation complaining about overbearing government, the main theme of the story is clear.

The next two paragraphs invite the reader's question:

How did it happen? Why? These are answered in what follows. It is a remarkable success in particularizing an intro on a whopping abstraction like the federal establishment.

No Precooked Dinners

The news story starts from an event. The feature story starts from an idea. "Let's do a story on the changes in Appalachia," the editor decides. "There haven't been any changes," the reporter discovers. "Fine, then let's do a story on why not. After all, the government poured millions into the place."

This is vague, but that's how it should be. Refining and massaging the idea is the outcome of, not the preliminary to, reporting. Neither you nor your editor can know in advance where the scent will lead you. It may go in unexpected directions. Writers who start with a detailed blueprint may have to tear it up — wasting time and energy. Some, God forbid, even prefabricate a lead or an intro. This is a form of prejudgment that handicaps you in two ways. First, you will restrict your reporting from the outset to sources and material that fit your preconceived thesis. You may miss a far better angle. Second, and worse, you may miss what's really important and thereby distort the truth.

Start your reporting and interviewing with an open mind. In time, and by dint of legwork and research, the story will assume a natural shape. You may have wanted, say, to do the Appalachian piece from the perspective of state officials and welfare workers who ladle out government aid. You may find that three old ladies who were among the first food stamp recipients, all of whose children worked in the mines, can open up richer vistas. The point is, stay loose until you have enough of a feel to decide that you have the right theme. At that phase, you'll be able to narrow your reporting to its requirements.

At first, though, cast your net wide. You never know what facts and details, peripheral when you haul them in, will turn into treasure when you write. The fact that the mine inspector is a rose fancier is worth little — until you discover that the mine operator he's dragged to court shares the floral passion and has been bested twice by the inspector in a state flower show. You won't get such piquant detail, which gives your story vitality, unless your questions and your curiosity range well beyond the reservation of the immediate subject.

Since you'll need to reconstruct a scene, recapture mood and atmosphere, you might do well to follow the cherished practice of AP's Hugh Mulligan, a longtime feature writer turned columnist: "I find it helpful to copy down emotions, observations and passing thoughts on how I feel about what I'm witnessing or hearing, mainly because I may never feel that way again when I sit down to write," he has said. "I take endless notes on everything I hear and see and smell and think or moon about."

Because most good feature writers amass a far greater hoard of material for every enterprise than they can use, writing becomes a great winnowing. Writers often can't bear to part with an anecdote, a character vignette, or a nosegay of facts that are amusing and interesting. But do they bear directly on the subject? If not, show them the door. Your profile of the single-minded engineer deals with his astonishing labors and the qualities of an infinitely precise mind that bring them about. His mother-in-law's odd experiences at a haunted house in Scotland are beguiling, but beside the point. Get rid of them. If you have three anecdotes illustrating the engineer's strange work habits, from midnight to eight in the morning, use the *one* that best makes the point. Don't belabor it with the others, however charming.

(As an example of a profile that gets its man with great economy of style, with all of its anecdotes and incidents strictly advancing its theme, read AP Special Correspondent Jules Loh's 600-word story on Big Six Henderson at the end of this chapter.)

This process of selection is the feature writer's purgatory. The good ones go through it with every story, though never cheerfully. How far the winnowing proceeds also depends on the editor's ukase on available space. Rebellions over such matters are not unheard of, but reasonable restrictions of wordage, besides being an inescapable fact of newspaper life, are a challenge rather than an inhibition. As Don Murray, former Boston newspaperman, now an English professor at the University of New Hampshire, put it: "Creativity is not the product of freedom, but the product of the conflict between freedom and discipline." The true craftsman can paint on a small canvas as fetchingly as on a large one.

Much agony can ensue from a craving to be definitive, which isn't the same as being thorough. Journalists, including feature writers, can never hope to say the last word on any subject. If you try that on a topic like nuclear power, or desegregation, or the genetic factor in intelligence, you're assailing Everest with your forehead. Limit yourself to a manageable slice of the subject. Your contribution will be the more valuable for it.

A feature story needs structure. Like the Red River, it can take all sorts of bends and curves, but it always stays within the banks. No offshoots flow from it. Readers should be able to follow it as if in a canoe, always curious about what's around the next bend.

Chronological Approach

Chronological narrative, which kept Scheherazade alive, is the simplest structure and often remarkably effective, particularly in reconstructing large events like the Mount

St. Helens eruption or the dark drama of the Peoples Temple.

While many features include chunks of chronology, it is usually modified by various devices. You may start in the middle of an action and use flashbacks. Always, you should spice straight chronology with foreshadowings — teasers, hints of what lies around the bend.

In a story on the 100th anniversary of Franklin D. Roosevelt's birth, for instance, Pett gave a largely chronological account of the president's mighty labors. But he framed the narrative in the experiences of two plain citizens whose lives had been greatly changed by the New Deal. (Direct tie-in with the present is a good practice in stories on historical subjects.) His format also gave Pett a human interest intro, leading from the two individuals to the affairs of state, and an ironic ending: one of those old New Dealers' sons had voted for Reagan.

Structure need not be elaborate. You can build some stories from scenes, more or less connected, with or without narrative transitions, each highlighting a significant episode. The "reporter's notebook" technique is a pleasant variant, informal and chatty, dipping rather than digging into a subject. It usually consists of separate items and vignettes, sketching various aspects of a place or event. The result can be highly readable, but success depends on sharp observation and good detail. And the pearls should be on a common strand, with some thematic relation among the items; you're not cleaning out the attic. (A fine example of the "reporter's notebook" device appears at the end of this chapter.)

AP's Sid Moody devised a novel structure for a profile of New Jersey. The story was a dazzling almanac of facts — historical, contemporary, statistical, out-of-the-way, plainly odd — interspersed at times with non-facts by way of humorous hyperbole. The format was a drive along the

New Jersey Turnpike, with Moody as the genial tour director, pausing at each exit to display the economic, physical and social landscape.

Here's how he began the story:

N.J. TURNPIKE (AP) — Standup comic: "Swine flu was discovered in New Jersey — where else?" (Laughter.)

Other Comic: "The Mafia is feeling the recession. They laid off four judges in Jersey." (More laughter.)

New Jersey today is an automatic boff, funnier than Brooklyn or downtown Burbank. The laughter emanates from the trillions of non-Jerseyans who cruise up the Turnpike staring at rear bumpers, dodging chemical trucks, sniffing refineries and gladly surrendering $1.50 to escape across the Hudson into New York.

It gets no respect. Yet Jersey gave America the steam locomotive (Hoboken, 1825); baseball (same place, 1846); football (New Brunswick, 1869); Edison's lightbulb (Menlo Park, 1879); movie cliffhangers (Palisades, early 1900s); the four-lane highway and cloverleaf (Newark); Count Basie; Valium; Meryl Streep; Allen Ginsberg; me and Secaucus. (Laughter.)

And it may become a pioneer in what to do, and what not to do, about rotted cities, dwindling farmland, aging suburbs, regional planning and local government. It may just be where the country is going.

New Jersey is 7.3 million people; 5 zillion pickups; sixth among the states in per capita income; 300-plus garbage dumps with Jimmy Hoffa buried in every one; 150,000 deer; 12 armored divisions of Mafioso; nine casinos; 16 skillion suburbs; 3,518 bartenders named Louie; one covered bridge; two U.S. senators, one a basketball player, the other convicted in the Abscam affair, and 40 of the state variety, three of them indicted. All of this acted out on a small stage.

A peek at the future? Turn off here, Exit 1.

Yup, that's a silo. We have 9,100 farms with about 1 million acres. They produce $2,977 per acre, tops in the nation. But half the farmland is owned by non-farmers. Read developers. Jersey farmers, average age 53, have a morale problem with subdivisions crowding right into the barnyard. The new suburbanites complain about chicken feathers on the front lawns, about missing trains because they got stuck behind an 8 mph tractor. The Garden State grows only 54 percent of its vegetables. Milk comes from Wisconsin. The farmers sell out and retire to Florida.

Belatedly, New Jersey thinks this is no solution.

Without following Moody all the way to Exit 9, you might note two things:

1. An avalanche of facts and figures doesn't necessarily smother a reader. Moody's cornucopia gives his piece a special charm. Moody (a persistent, if flawed, trombonist on the side) is aware that sometimes there is music in mathematical preciseness.

2. The fifth paragraph performs a valuable service, crystallizing the significance of the story by relating New Jersey's condition to the nation at large. All sizable features benefit from such a "pregnant paragraph" high in the story, telling the reader: "Here's what's important (or unusual) about the story. Read on."

You may have caught Moody sneaking in a first person pronoun ("me and Secaucus"). Fine for this occasion as another humorous aside. But in general, leave the perpendicular pronoun to the columnists. The exceptions are rare — stories in which the writer tells about an expressly personal experience, perhaps overcoming a debilitating illness or surviving three weeks in the Amazon garlanded with anacondas.

People are by definition human interest, or at least human, and profiles are a staple of feature output. They range from the full-fledged portrait of 2,000 words to more cursory sketches of someone in the news.

Don't cram a profile with routine biographical detail; keep that for the obit. Look for the characteristics, habits, traits, working methods and experiences that make your subject different.

In short profiles of "personalities in the news," it's a good idea to concentrate on qualities that got them there. If you're dealing with a person who's just ascended to high office in a major corporation, pick anecdotes, quotes and background details that help explain the success.

When you can, relate details and color to the main theme: *She picks her clothes with the discriminating eye developed in six years as the company's leading buyer. In her gardening — her main avocation — she's as organized and meticulous as she's said to be in running the new division.*

Routine profile interviews of celebrities tend to be the least promising. That's because celebrities are acutely media-conscious, forever intent on their, Lord help them, "image." They have stock answers to all the usual questions and become vague or tongue-tied at unusual ones. They like people. They think the city they're in is wonderful. They like sports. They like music. They like babies. They like mothers. They think love is wonderful. They adore walking in the rain. They find everything a challenge. They are, in fact, animated clichés.

The only hope is to get such people to talk about their one vein of expertise or enthusiasm, if any; the actress may be interesting on acting techniques, the schlock author on how he trip-hammers his epics together.

The value of steering people in interviews to subjects with which they have real affinity and thorough familiarity is often overlooked. Ask a plumber or a microbiologist about politics, theology or current affairs, and you'll usually get regurgitated opinions as fascinating as the telephone book.

Let them discourse about the ins and outs of plumbing or microbiology and they're apt to wax voluble, enthusiastic and downright informative. Such stuff, even when slightly technical, usually is interesting even to readers without passion for pipe wrenches or electron microscopes.

Profiles of Very Important Citizens often require great effort to avoid the puffery fed you by the handiest sources — assorted aides, associates, flunkeys. Tapping Wilbur Lickspittle Jr. for quotes about his boss, Jarvis Housingstart, the Biggest Builder in the West, is unlikely to prove revealing. Balancing Lickspittle's fawning testimonial with the bleats of tenants at Housingstart Heights, where the roof recently blew off in a mild breeze, won't necessarily get you closer to the real Housingstart. You need sources who know him well but are neither beholden nor harbor a vendetta. It takes work.

Where Solemnity Palls

A sense of humor, an eye for irony, and a light touch are formidable assets. You're thrice blessed if you have them. Not every subject can be treated lightly, but none calls for stodgy solemnity. The feature, after all, is intended to please as well as inform. A certain playfulness of style is seldom out of place. Pett's epic on the bureaucracy, as you saw from the earlier sample, was relaxed and informal for all of its weightiness of subject.

Here's another example of Pett in full cry:

NEW YORK (AP) — He is the freshest thing to blossom in New York since chopped liver, a mixed metaphor of a politician, the antithesis of the packaged leader, irrepressible, candid, impolitic, spontaneous, funny, feisty, independent, uncowed by voter blocs, unsexy, unhandsome, unfashionable and altogether charismatic, a man oddly at peace with himself in an unpeaceful place, a mayor who presides over the country's largest Babel with unseemly joy.

Clearly, an original. Asked once what his weaknesses were, Ed Koch said that for the life of him he couldn't think of any. "I like myself," he said.

The streets are still dirty. The subways are still unsafe. The specter of bankruptcy is never further away than next year's loan. But Edward Irwin Koch, who runs the place like a Jewish mother with no fear of the rich relatives, appears to be the most popular mayor of this implausible town since Fiorello LaGuardia more than a generation ago.

Yes, yes, elsewhere I extol the short sentence and especially the short lead, and this one runs 65 words. Which only means that when a good writer breaks a rule for good reason, it works. Anyway, the reader is having fun.

Poetic License Forbidden

Feature writing, as that lead demonstrates, offers greater latitude than straight news writing. It thrives on color, nuance, wit, fancy, emotive words, dialogue, character. Feature writers, like novelists, have many literary devices to engage readers emotionally, and that's their privilege.

But freedom, as has often been noted, entails responsibility. Feature writers must be accurate and scrupulously fair.

What you say happened must have happened in precisely that way. Frolic with words, enjoy yourself (if any writer can), but remember there's no poetic or literary license when it comes to facts. Repeat that to yourself every morning.

Fairness is more difficult to pinpoint, but a person can be sandbagged in many ways by the techniques in the feature writer's armory — through selection of details, through invidious description, through the use of adjectives and even through the setting of a scene.

That doesn't mean that every anecdote that presents a subject in an unfavorable light must be balanced by a favorable one, or that every critical comment must be offset by a burst of praise. Fairness is not a matter of arithmetic.

It does mean that feature writers, as honest reporters, recognize that life is multi-dimensional, that motives are often ambiguous, that moral judgments are beyond their purview, that a one-sided portrayal, whether of a person or an institution, is a sin even less pardonable than shoddy technique.

Artists at Work

The best way to learn feature writing, or any writing, is to read — study — the work of those who know their business. I've drawn heavily on some of them in this section.

What follows is a small selection of features that repay reading and illustrate some of the points discusssed. I wish space permitted a fuller representation.

The first is a story by the late Hal Boyle, irreplaceable dean of the AP Poets' Corner, reporter, Pulitzer Prize winner, war correspondent, columnist, master of the simple declarative sentence. The story is about the birth and death of a calf. Technically, it is a fine example of the power of understatement and of precise visual detail.

The second is a short profile of a retired revenue agent, by Jules Loh. It is obvious from the chosen material that Loh could have written at twice the length; he chose a smaller canvas. Note the economy of language. Every sentence is pertinent to the theme, every word tells.

The third is from *The New York Times* by AP alumnus John Vinocur. It shows what can be done with the "reporter's notebook" format, in this case a collection of items about Bonn at Christmas time. Lightly, but precisely, Vinocur not only provides interesting reading on the flavor of the West German capital but says much about its politics and culture.

They represent different categories of features, but note what all three have in common. Each is free of mannerisms, verbal flourishes, literary tinsel. Each is written with simplicity, clarity, taste. Each demonstrates the unassailable essential: good feature writing proceeds from good reporting.

Read and enjoy.

LIFE AND DEATH IN A COW BARN
By HAL BOYLE

LONG VALLEY, N.J. (AP) — It was an ordinary Sunday outside the big, cool dairy barn. The dressed up people came and went to church, the less dressed up people from the city enjoyed the sunny countryside.

Inside the big, cool dairy barn it was even more of an ordinary day. Cows have no Sunday. The daily drama of life and death among the herd went on unchanged except for one thing.

There was a young girl present who saw the drama for the first time. The events of the day changed her, perhaps forever.

The three cows involved were numbered 204 and 140 and 219 — and the first was old and through, the second was young and having her first calf, and the third was middle-aged and having maybe her third or fourth calf.

No. 204 was at the head of the barn and lying, too weary to get up, at the front of the barn with her head in its stanchion. She was 14, very old for a cow. Her milk had fleshed a thousand distant children she had never seen. But now she lay there, unprotestingly, waiting for the slaughterer's truck to come and take her away.

During the morning, No. 140, the young heifer, delivered her first calf after a rugged ordeal. Worn out by the struggle and oblivious to the responsibilities of motherhood, she wandered away from her sprawling, weak, tan calf.

A group of summer residents who came down to see the calf found that No. 219, the middle-aged cow, had taken up the duties of the confused young mother. She was carefully and methodically cleaning the sprawling calf with her tongue, as animals do.

Suddenly it became apparent the middle-aged cow's own ordeal of maternity was at hand. One of the men turned to a young girl, his niece, and said:

"If you're going to get back to the city before the traffic ties you up, you'd better leave now."

"I've never seen anything born before," she said. "I want to stay."

"But it may be hours," he said. "You can't tell."

"Just for a little while," she pleaded. "Then I'll be off."

Her uncle and the others left and the young girl was alone in the filtered light of the barn, sweet with the deep rich scent of hay and animal bodies. Old cow No. 204, a factory worn out, glanced at her with the idle and placid disinterest of age.

The young girl knelt beside No. 219. The miracle of approaching birth made the two one. She knit her fingers and tugged at them tensely in unconscious rhythm with the laboring cow.

"Please," she whispered. "Try again, harder."

All at once they were three — or almost three. The calf was half-born. Then something was wrong.

"Please, please, please!" cried the girl. She heard a noise. Two dairy hands had come into the far end of the dairy barn.

"Quick!" she cried. "The calf is strangling."

The two men ran up. One grabbed a rope. With it they completed the rough obstetrics of the farm, and the calf was delivered, its fore-hooves raised to its muzzle in the posture of prayer.

The calf lay there — warm, wet and motionless. One workman bent and wiped its muzzle to clear the nostrils, then massaged its ribs in an attempt at artifical respiration. The calf lay still.

"But I saw its eyes move," said the girl. "If I could have called you in time. . ."

The rough workmen looked at her, puzzled. A calf is $20, more or less, and they come often on a big dairy farm.

"I don't think so," said one of the men, not unkindly. "These things happen, you know."

As one of the men dragged the dead calf away, mother cow No. 219 let out a bellow of anguish that had a human ring of despair in it, and crashed into a chain barrier. She wandered about wildly for a moment, then lowered her head and again began licking the living calf of cow No. 140, the bewildered young heifer who hadn't yet risen to the chores of motherhood.

The young girl got into her car.

"But I saw its eyes move," she said, half crying. "If I could have just. . ."

She turned the car and headed it toward the city. She had seen the sadness of death taking life at the portal of birth, and she would always remember this Sunday, just another ordinary day on a busy farm.

BIG SIX HENDERSON
By JULES LOH

LOUISVILLE, Ky. (AP) — In Kentucky's moonshine hollows, one name still strikes awe: Big Six Henderson.

Big Six Henderson busted up more stills in his time than anybody in history. If that is not so, at least it is the legend. When moonshiners talk about Big Six Henderson, the line between truth and legend blurs.

"I don't know what the record is," Big Six Henderson allowed, thinking back on his days of prowling around in alien corn.

"I know I raided more than 5,000 stills and sent more than 5,600 moonshiners to prison. You could figure it up. I've kept a copy of my daily reports for every day I was a revenue agent."

That was for a span of 28 years until he retired a few years ago, and it figures up to roughly a still every other day. The saga of Big Six Henderson, though, is hardly told in dry statistics.

The moonshiners Big Six Henderson tracked down imparted heroic dimensions to him and respected him as much as they feared him.

"Mr. Big Six," one woman said when he came to haul her husband off to jail for a third time, "we're proud to have folks know we know you." More than a few moonshiners named their children for Big Six Henderson.

One even named his mash barrel for him, painted "Big Six" on it and talked to it fondly.

"Good morning, Big Six," he said to the barrel one day. "Why don't we just run ourselves off a little batch, you and I. What do you say to that, Big Six?"

"That you're caught, Thurlow," Big Six Henderson said, stepping out of the mist.

At 75, Big Six Henderson is still impressive to behold.

He is a bear of a man, 6-foot-4, with a thick bush of white hair and eyes the color of wet turquoise. His mother named him William; Big Six was the name he picked up when he was going to law school and throwing a baseball after the fashion of Christy "Big Six" Mathewson.

His career as a lawyer was as rapid as his fastball.

"My first and only case was defending a guy who broke into a warehouse. He was guilty as hell, but I got him off. I decided if I had to make a living that way I might as well be a holdup man and at least be honest about it."

There is nothing complicated about Big Six Henderson's sense of justice.

So he became a federal treasury agent, a "revenooer" as they are known in the hills, and went about it with a single-mindedness that became the stuff of myth.

Big Six Henderson can smell a still from 10 miles off. "Actually about two miles if the wind is right," Big Six Henderson corrected.

Big Six Henderson can shoot a pistol out of your hand at a hundred yards. "Well, the way that got started was by accident. I was aiming at the man's belt buckle."

It was no myth, though, that he could creep through the woods as quiet as smoke in his green raiding suit and could run like a deer for miles. Usually he didn't have to run after his quarry.

"Homer, halt!" he shouted at one fleeing moonshiner. The man froze in his tracks.

"I'm halted, Big Six, I'm halted."

He was a legend in his time, all right, and not just because of his uncanny skill and his zealotry. He also had a reputation for fair play and decent treatment of the moonshiners he caught.

"I never regarded them as doing something evil, just illegal," Big Six Henderson said, "and I never abused them." The big man thumbed through a sheaf of his faded daily reports, looking wistfully at the names.

"Killed a few, but never abused them."

'TIS THE SEASON WHEN BONN HIBERNATES
By JOHN VINOCUR
Special to The New York Times

BONN, Dec. 24 — Scott and Zelda would have had their problems here. Bonn offers little romance, few parties, a premium on solemnity, and considerable discomfort with passion of any kind.

The ferries across the Rhine quit at 10. The little underground train, a half-dozen stops in a straight line, shuts down at 12. If the Fitzgeralds, somehow transported to the riverside between the Chancellery and the Bundestag, stood at night listening for the pounding of the German soul, searching the black currents for a clue to the writhings at the heart of Europe, what they would get back is the clicking sound of stoplights on carless streets, and a view of barges dragging cement to Mülheim or Neuss, an outtake from an industrial short.

That's most of the year. The weeks before and after Christmas are different. Arguably comatose under normal circumstances, the capital of West Germany, pop. 283,000, slides into deeper, stiller quietude from Dec. 22 till the second week of January.

With its politicians gone, the Government's flotilla of Mercedes sedans garaged for the interval, and most of the foreign diplomatic corps dispersed, Bonn feels rather like the campus of a small theological school between semesters. Only the townies are left, and what the Germans call the Stallwacht — the stable guard assigned to watch the horses while the lords are at play.

●

Helmut Schmidt took off last weekend, without lighting a Christmas tree or chucking a chin. He'll be back the third week in January. The scene at the Chancellery today was almost perfect stasis. There was a single dirty raincoat on the coat rack in the lobby and a single doorkeeper listening to traffic reports from Baden-Württemberg.

Mr. Schmidt, who rather likes being called a pragmatist, was obviously in no mood to dawdle in a town where little more could be accomplished. And without him, the ultimate 14-hour-workday symbol, why should anyone else stay around, expecting to get something done?

•

Giacomo Casanova stayed in Bonn in 1760, a party guest at the residence of the Prince elector of Cologne. Casanova reports dancing the forlana to near exhaustion. He also acknowledges having been less than diplomatic and giving several kisses to a lady dressed up as a milkmaid. Since then, the party scene has gone straight downhill.

Young couples, both German and foreign, who come to live in Bonn for a time and who think Munich or Paris could be remade around their dinner table with local Scotts and Zeldas, tend to get disappointed fast. Bonn has bureaucrats, diplomats and journalists, but no admen, stewardesses, p.r. guys, industrialists, soccer players, demimondaines, literati or elegant layabouts. Flash, big money and wild talk are scarce. After a year or so of bucking the town's constraints, the ambitious new arrivals tend to accept them, join the formal reception lines, drink the white wine and go home early.

In some cities, there is a series of parties before Christmas that has a specially cheerful, exciting momentum. In Bonn the process is reversed; the parties, mostly diplomatic or official, are a repetition of all the others during the year, but increasingly bland because the politicians drift away as the holiday approaches. Since most members of Parliament don't bring their wives or families with them to Bonn, and most go home from Thursday night to Monday morning, the guests are inevitably mostly men, holding glasses, who have already seen each other three times that day. The conversation is always politics, small talk not being one of the great German gifts.

One of the men holding a glass last week was Karsten Vogt, a Social Democratic legislator from Frankfurt, where his wife works as an architect. She never comes to Bonn. The reason, she tells her husband, is "you and your boring friends."

Mr. Vogt takes off before 9, the way everyone else does. He goes home to a small dormitory-type apartment provided by the Government, which is presumably what most of the other legislators do. Bonn's sedation wins: in 31 years of postwar democracy, it has made for early bedtimes and a readiness to accept long floor debates and endless party caucuses.

Occasionally, there is a man feeling trapped in Bonn who insists the party must go on. Last week, Leo Wagner, a former member of Parliament from Bavaria, was found guilty of obtaining about $150,000 by fraud, money he needed to pay off bills he ran up in the nightclubs of Cologne, about a half-hour's drive from the capital. Perhaps in the spirit of Christmas, perhaps because he knew Bonn well, the judge gave Mr. Wagner an 18-month suspended sentence.

●

There are, of course, many defenders of the city, including some effective ones. The most powerful intellectual argument is not to seek from Bonn what it cannot offer. Be content with its stillness, the argument runs. For the holders of this thesis, the hushed weeks around Christmas are an exalted, exquisite vacuum.

●

The people who are left behind during the holidays, the Stallwacht and the townies, deal with the silence as best they can, although one of the stable guard, recalling a phrase from the arguments of a defense lawyer for a terrorist, insisted such a degree of sensory deprivation would be actionable if he only had the legal status of a bona fide prisoner. The stable guard, according to some, tend to pass time reading, although the lead stories on the local pages of the city's serious daily newspaper have reached the level of "Norwegians dance around the Christmas tree" and "Star of the snake show: the cobra."

The townies — Beethoven was born here — seem imperturbable. There is no sign that they noticed Karl Marx, a student in Bonn, or made a great fuss over Adolf Hitler, a frequent visitor to the Hotel Dreesen, from where he stared at the Rhine.

Alexander M. Klieforth, a former American diplomat here and an officer in the United States Army unit that captured Bonn in World War II, has told of setting up an artillery position in a park next to the river on a Sunday in March 1945. Ignoring the cannons, crowds of strollers insisted on walking through the park, getting in the way of the big guns. Mr. Klieforth erected a sign that read: "Während des Feuergefechts darf diese Anlage nicht betreten werden" — "During the exchange of fire, this area may not be entered."

There's a fair chance that the descendants of the people who did not notice the noise are not much disturbed by the quiet either.

USAGE: Handling Those Hectoring Hangups

10

Split 'N' Polish

Split infinitives were good enough for William Shakespeare, George Bernard Shaw and a flock of other capable writers. They should be good enough for the rest of us.

Shaw, in fact, once complained to a newspaper about the harrumphings of an anti-splitter.

"Your fatuous specialist," GBS fumed, "is now beginning to rebuke 'second rate' newspapers for using such phrases as 'to suddenly go' and 'to boldly say.' I ask you, sir, to put this man out without interfering with his perfect freedom of choice to suddenly go, to go suddenly, and suddenly to go. Try an intelligent Newfoundland dog in his place."

Split in peace then, but split for good reason: When it sounds better, and when it's to avoid ambiguity.

Some perfectly good splits:

> He said he had great difficulty *to really understand* what the government was up to.

Try to put the adverb *really* elsewhere in the sentence without disruption.

The cops wanted those youngsters *to really see* the danger.

Painless split, increases emphasis.

They said they would try *to carefully dislodge* the tangle of twisted girders tomorrow.

Smooth enough. *Carefully to dislodge* **is impossible, and** *to dislodge carefully* **doesn't sound right.**
On the other hand, there's no point in splitting the infinitive here:

The company hopes *to substantially increase* profits.

. . . *increase profits substantially* **gets the nod. From the ear.**

Avoid splitting an infinitive with two or more words:

He said he planned to energetically and devotedly pursue those objectives.

Adverbs after *objectives,* **or: . . .** *to pursue those objectives with energy and devotion.*

They promised to at all times obey the law of the land.

They promised at all times to obey the law of the land **is possible, but . . .** *law of the land at all times* **seems preferable.**

One way to not split an infinitive is with *not, never* **or** *always,* **which go more naturally beforehand:**

The mayor asked strikers *to not insist* on the march (*not to insist*).

The president made sure *to always receive* his visitors at the entrance (*always made sure to*).

At the meeting, he advised parents *to never let* the youngsters walk alone (*never to let*).

I hope this is enough to somewhat clear the air.

Genderly Speaking

The point can't be overemphasized: words must fit together naturally, comfortably, so they do not distract the
reader by calling attention to themselves. In the effort to
rid the language of male bias — a commendable effort —
distraction often results. Nowhere is the straining for fairness more contrived than in the juggling of personal pronouns.

> The mayor warned every homeowner that he or she is responsible
> for clearing the snow in front of his or her house.

The writer didn't want to imply that all homeowners are
male, so instead he danced awkwardly around the problem,
kicking up clouds of clutter. In this case, and all like it, the
solution is easy. Recast the sentence to use the sexually
neutral plural pronoun:

> The mayor warned all homeowners that they are responsible for
> clearing the snow in front of their houses.

The baby who sucks his thumb can as clearly and naturally be written *Babies who suck their thumbs. A reporter
tries to protect his sources* can, eliminating bias, become
Reporters try to protect their sources.

But what if there is no graceful way around the singular
pronoun? Should the sentence two paragraphs back have
said *he or she danced awkwardly around the problem,* or,
almost as clumsily, repeated *the writer* instead of using the
pronoun *he?*

I say no. So does the AP *Stylebook.* Avoid presumptions
of maleness whenever possible. Be especially alert for such
constructions as *the boss ... he* which imply that only
males are bosses. At the same time, avoid straining for neu-
trality through constructions that jar and call attention to
themselves. Let good judgment tell you whether it is a case

of a permissible *he* or a case of presumed maleness that should be avoided.

As for nouns, apply the same rule. When the choice is a natural one — *reporter* for *newsman, firefighter* for *fireman, worker* for *workingman, mail carrier* for *mailman* — use the word that includes both sexes. But avoid manufactured contrivances such as *spokesperson.*

Substitutions: Terminal and Incipient

The old superstition, based on a grammatical fallacy, that no sentence should end with a preposition, is happily dying out. For that matter, most good writers down the ages have ignored it.

Police recovered the bloody ax he killed her with is good English, whereas *Police recovered the bloody ax with which he killed her* is stodgy.

As Winston Churchill said, it's a "pedantry up with which we will not put."

Some traditionalists also cling to another myth: Sentences must not start with *and* or *but.* No reason why they shouldn't, though in practice it's often overdone. Look over the initial *ands* and *buts* you write. And see if they are superfluous, as the *and* is in this sentence.

But implies a contrast, and for that reason — not because of its position — it is wrong here:

> The defendant appeared dejected by his wife's outburst. But the prosecutor indicated he might recall her later.

An *and* would be possible, but actually neither is needed.

It's All Relative

Careful writers insist on correct use of the relative pronouns *that* and *which* not merely out of respect for syntax but in the cause of clarity. The two words are used in restrictive and non-restrictive clauses, respectively, and are not interchangeable. The following two sentences do not mean the same thing:

> The bicycle that was on the porch was stolen.

> The bicycle which was on the porch was stolen.

The first sentence leaves the implication that of several bicycles, the one that was stolen was the one on the porch. The second sentence provides the non-essential fact of the theft that the stolen bicycle happened to be on the porch.

RULE: Use *which* for non-defining, non-limiting clauses; use *that* for clauses that define.

Here is a way to remember. If you could put the clause in parenthesis or set it off with commas, use *which*. If the clause is necessary to full understanding, use *that*.

> The stream, which [by the way] rises dangerously during the flood season, flows near the village.

> The stream that rises dangerously during the flood season [as opposed to other streams] flows near the village.

Legalism

And/or is something that lawyers seem to enjoy and it's one of those happy turns that makes legal forms so attractive.

Leave it to them. It's always avoidable:

> The officers thought they would find the loot and/or other evidence at the scene. (Either *and* or *or* but not both.)

> The force was to consist of National Guardsmen and/or state police. (National Guardsmen or state police or both.)

Attorneys, in the ritual of avoiding leading questions and/or (chuckle) the appearance of prejudgment, fling themselves at *if any*. Some news writers are impressed by the sound, though it's rarely sensible in copy:

> There was a question what effect, if any, the company proposal would have on the rank and file.

Since the proposal was bound to have some effect, omit *if any*. If you want to quibble about that, there is still another way: *If the proposal would have any effect . . .*

Here's a case where a reporter was more lawyerly than the lawyers:

> None of the lawyers involved would say what legal strategy, if any, they would take.

Candidates for disbarment, I'd say, if there's a chance that they would not adopt any legal strategy.

Subjunctivitis

Writers sometimes tense up over things that haven't happened, though they have, and flee into the woulds.

> Still, McEnroe did not concede the third set. As he *would say* later, he had opportunities to win throughout the match.

There's nothing incorrect about the subjunctive construction, but why not make it *as he said afterward*?

The woulds thicken menacingly in this lead:

> MEXIA, Texas — The party would go on all night. But at 11 p.m., as the festivities were just gathering steam, the drownings that would mar memories of the day and create a furor whose tremors would reach Washington were about to happen.

That lead creates an eerie backward-forward-not yet effect, and it isn't helped by the dreadful gulf between *drownings* and *were about to happen*.

The following gets us out of the time warp:

> MEXIA, Texas — The party went on all night and was just gathering steam when the drownings occurred. Later, the tragedy marred the memories of the day and raised a furor whose tremors reached Washington.

If the extended subjunctive seems a clumsy way to grapple with the future, the fatuous backward glance seems even worse. This makes much too much of the fact that the future is unknowable:

> Little did Joe Smith know, when he peered shortsightedly at the blackboard in first grade, that he would some day be Smithtown's leading ophthalmologist.

That is a hypothetical example, but representative. Here is an actual example from a newspaper:

> When Sidney Sheldon was writing his latest best seller, he probably had no idea it would be used as a challenge by those who have been saying that the Washington County library in Abingdon is loaded with dirty books.

The absurdity is compounded by the cautious *probably*.

You would do well to avoid the subjunctive if you can, and to leave speculative flashbacks alone altogether.

Dash It All

A lot of writers like to toss around dashes to keep things stirred up. They look, well, more dashing than the crooked little comma, the hang-dog semicolon and the obese parenthesis, for all of which dashes are frequently misused.

The comma indicates a slight break in the thought of a sentence; the semicolon a rather larger one, and the dash an abrupt, dramatic turn. Dashes, therefore, should be used sparingly; overuse weakens their effect. They often add a jarring note to an otherwise smooth sentence.

The dash is used correctly here:

> They trudged wearily along the trail — dozens had died on it, and they knew it — until they made camp utterly exhausted.

But not in the following examples:

> He said his grandmother — who had just reached 93 — was a "very vigorous old lady."

No abrupt break in the thought. Commas instead of dashes.

> The defendant said he hadn't known she had left — without explanation.

Fake dramatics. . . . *had left without explanation.*

> The 4,372-piece set — an average $48 per piece — had arrived at the White House by truck from the Lenox China plant . . .

Parentheses or commas.

> Their arrival meant that suburbia — which had sprawled slowly across North Jersey since the 1930s — had finally pierced the state's westernmost farming country.

Commas.

> The burden of clerical rule — including the banning of alcoholic beverages, Western music and movies; requirements that women be veiled, and Islamic punishments, including death for what are deemed sexual offenses — has fallen most heavily on the Westernized, the educated, and the middle class.

The dash must have looked to the writer as the only way to save this sentence. Had he tried parentheses or commas, he might have realized that he needed to go back to the drawing board.

Lay On, MacDuff

Despite the twanging testimony of country singers, it is possible to use *lie* and *lay* correctly.

I suspect the confusion stems from the fact that *to lay,* meaning "to place something on a surface," is also the past tense of *to lie,* meaning "to recline." To make matters worse, *to lie* is also the verb which means "to tell a falsehood," an inflammatory word which may cause some to flinch and use *lay,* incorrectly, in its place.

Lay aside, for a moment, the falsehood meaning of "lie"

and concentrate on the two verbs that are so often confused. Start with the principal parts:

Verb 1 — lie, lay, lain.

Verb 2 — lay, laid, laid.

> The derelict stumbled to the park to *lie* on a bench. He selected the same bench that he *lay* on yesterday. He has *lain* on the same bench every night for the past week.
>
> He looked for a place to *lay* his knapsack. He *laid* it beside the bench in the same place as yesterday, the same place he has *laid* it for a week.

Remember: *to lay* takes an object; *to lie* does not.

Et Cetera

At the end of a sentence containing a string of words or phrases separated by commas, writers sometimes feel compelled to attach a meaningless little tail designed to tell the reader, "This is an incomplete list."

> The adult education program offers a wide variety of courses, such as woodworking, French cookery, creative writing and origami, *among others.*
>
> He stays active during his leisure hours with golf, carpentry, bird watching, fishing, hiking *and similar activities.*

There's a way out of that hangup. In the first example, delete the *and* before the final item on the list and insert a comma: . . . *cooking, creative writing, origami.* In the second example, just cross out *and similar activities.*

The simple trick of omitting *and* before the final item in a list suggests it is an incomplete list. Read it aloud and you will see.

Numbers Game

Numbers go into stories for precision. The way they're often handled, though, makes them sorry figures — vague and confusing enough to have readers muttering to them-selves.

Let us count the ways:

1. The More-Less Seesaw

Johnson got *more* than $100,000 *less* than he expected.

First, try to get an exact figure. (We hide too often be-hind approximations.) Failing, write it this way: *Johnson expected at least $100,000 more than he got.*

Fewer than the more than 60,000 ticketholders showed up.

At least 60,000 bought tickets, but not all of them showed up.

The staff of the state Utilities Commission recommended a $4.7 million rate hike for Carolina Telephone & Telegraph Co. But the recommended figure is *more than* $21 million *less than* the company expected.

I suspect one more phone call would have gotten the re-porter the exact sum. Otherwise, *at least* is again the way out.

2. Mathematical Leads

A jury of four men and eight women deliberated more than 21 hours before convicting a 19-year-old high school dropout of killing his 18-year-old girlfriend two years ago.

Too much. Stats-happy sportswriters also are prone to throw these curve balls:

The rangy, 6-foot-6 forward who just turned 20 scored 22 points to Tibbets' 18 as the Jays pulled out the game with eight seconds to go for their 10th straight victory. They had trailed 34-33 at halftime.

KANSAS CITY, Mo. — Nick Lowery kicked field goals of 20, 20, 42 and 41 yards Sunday, leading Kansas City . . .

3. Bottomless Pit.

The company's losses could total up to $11 million . . .

Or as little as $2.50? Try to give the range: *Could lose from $6 million to $11 million.*

4. Math Test

When they first met, Mr. Klipstein was nearly twice the younger man's age.

And how much was that? Klipstein's age was given five grafs earlier. The younger man's age was never given.

This was about two-thirds the amount they spent for food.

This story made the reader backtrack four grafs to find the food budget, then figure the two-thirds.

5. Execrable Approximations

About, almost and other fudges are sometimes necessary (don't write *approximately* or *some*) but they're best used with round figures only.

About 112 policemen were sent to the scene of the disturbance.

Again, the best solution is *at least.*

More than 13 people were in the group, and police seized *some* three.

The reader wonders why the reporter couldn't have gotten such a low count right. Otherwise, fall back on *at least.*

And don't say *about* when the number is exact and should be ascertained for the story: ... *who handles newsprint purchases for the Gannett group of about 80 newspapers.* No. Use the exact number. To do otherwise is just lazy.

6. Do the Arithmetic

When editing a story with numbers in it, doublecheck the writer's arithmetic. If the story enumerates groups of various sizes, for example, make sure the numbers total the figure in the lead. In short, do the math.

That's That

Some sentences read well without *that,* others don't. There's no rule about when to put it in. It is true, though, that you can never go wrong by including it, while you can cause small disturbances by omitting it.

No problem with the absence of *that* in these sentences:

> The commissioner said she was sure they would comply.

> The secretary disclosed he would leave for Paris tomorrow.

There's something wrong with the following, however:

> Mayor Koch said years ago, the city had tried this method of financing but had failed.

That reads at first blush as though the mayor had said it years ago. *That* after *said* would have been better.

> He said in a survey of state motels by the state association, it was discovered . . .

Again, *that* after said. He didn't say it in a survey.

You must always use *that* when the word following a verb may be wrongly construed as its object:

> The teacher reported the children who threw the books would be disciplined.

> The committee vote signaled the bill stands a good chance of passing.

Without *that* after *reported* in the first example and *signaled* in the second, you have the teacher reporting the children and the vote signaling the bill. The reader is momentarily misled. Insert *that* after the verb to keep the meaning clear and the writing smooth.

It's usually better to use *that* when a time element comes between the verb and the *that* clause:

> The agency said today it will have additional shipments en route
> . . .

Slightly awkward, and the *today* may be briefly taken to refer to the shipments.

> Stephens said he would like to seek a compromise with Williams before taking the bill up in his committee because he believes the House of Delegates would approve the bill as before, but it is of little value if it is destined to die in the Senate.

This seems to require a *that* after the *but,* since the clause otherwise reads like the reporter's comment. A *that* in this second clause would also call for a *that* after *said.* A *but that* or *and that* in the second clause needs a parallel *that* in the first.

What's in It for Me?

Science writers and others on specialty beats know that part of their job is to translate — to reduce the vocabulary of, say, genetic engineering to lay terms. Covering legislatures and government usually doesn't entail such mysteries, but there are other hangups. Jargon, dealt with elsewhere, is one. So is an obsession with mechanics.

A common pitfall for legislative reporters is the notion that readers share the insider's passion for procedural detail and political shadow boxing. What readers want to know, right off the bat, is what's in it for them — the practical consequences. Legislative coverage and other governmental reporting that loses sight of this is writing tailored to the reporter's pressroom pals, cloakroom pols and agency moles.

Something important no doubt was happening in the following, but how much reader interest survives the approach?

> WASHINGTON — The Carter administration is about to take its second major step in governmental reorganization. But the new agency, while reducing the government payroll, will increase the government budget.
>
> On Saturday, the United States Information Agency and the State Department's Bureau of Educational and Cultural Affairs will merge to form the International Communications Agency.
>
> The new agency will have about the same number of employees, roughly 8,700, as now work in its two components.
>
> Its requested budget for fiscal 1979 is $413 million, as opposed to a combined budget of $348 million for the two agencies that are, in a technical sense, going out of existence.

The Federal Register couldn't have put it more compellingly.

Note in the next example how blurry the one point of reader interest becomes under inconsequential mechanics:

> BOSTON — The Massachusetts Legislature has finalized action on a bill providing for a public vote in the November election on the question of repealing the state's Sunday closing laws.
>
> By a voice vote, the Senate enacted the bill Monday and sent it to the governor.
>
> The last obstacle to the enactment of the bill was removed when the House, on a 178-33 roll call, voted not to reconsider its enactment of the bill several weeks ago.

> BOSTON — The Massachusetts Legislature has decided to give voters a chance to say whether they want the state's blue laws repealed.
>
> Under those ancient statutes, dating back to colonial days, most businesses must be closed on Sunday.
>
> The voters' verdict in November will not be binding on the Legislature. Business generally favors repeal, while some unions oppose it.
>
> The Senate passed the bill setting up the referendum and

The measure provides for a non-binding referendum on the blue laws, which require that most business activity cease on Sunday.

sent it to the governor Monday. A move to block the measure in the House failed.

The right-hand version focuses on the substance of the legislation, while the original emphasizes procedure at needless length.

BISMARCK, N.D. — The 44th Legislative Assembly convenes Tuesday for the opening of what most legislative leaders have called one of the most important sessions in the state's history.

Few care what legislative leaders call it. More to the point was material that didn't come up until the fourth paragraph:

BISMARCK, N.D. — The Legislative Assembly opening Tuesday will have to deal with the largest budget in North Dakota history and grapple with decisions about coal development in the western part of the state.

The following was intended mainly as a human (or animal) interest story. Why encumber the lead with legislative detail?

WASHINGTON — Members of a House-Senate conference committee agreed today on a legislative package for western ranges that includes provisions for giving away wild horses and burros to anyone willing to care for the animals.

WASHINGTON — If you want a wild horse or a burro, just promise you'll take good care of it and it's yours, courtesy of Congress.

In short, don't put the cart before the burro.

BESTIARY: A Compendium for the Careful and the Crotchety

11

Standards of written English are not rigid. Some usages blossom briefly and die; others take root and enrich the language. The process is slow and unpredictable. Meanwhile, careful users of the language often disagree on this or that locution.

That said, what follows here is a collection of usages which I regard as bestial. (In the matter of misuse of words, I allow myself to overstate.) Some of the entries, at this stage in the development of the language, allow for no argument. If you write *dis*interested when you mean *un*interested you are wrong, period. Other entries, I admit, may be open to discussion — but not if I'm handling the copy. Every editor has crotchets. Among these are some of mine.

A BEFORE H.   Unless you're prepared to write *an* horse, *an* ham, or *an* hamburger, make it *a* historian, *a* historical or *a* hysterical moment. The initial *H* in those words is pronounced, or rather aspirated, unlike in *hour* or *honest,* which take *an.*

ACTIVE CONSIDERATION.   Have you ever heard of anybody giving a plan or proposal passive consideration? This is bureaucratic baloney meant to sound grander than *thinking it over.*

AD HOC.   In Latin, it means "toward this." An *ad hoc* committee is one appointed to deal with one particular case or problem. Officialdom loves to go off ad hocked, and so does the business world. But why? If you write, *The league appointed a committee to oversee the flower show,* the *ad hoc* is understood. Or you could say, *a special committee.* Use something other than *ad hoc* — at least *pro tem.*

ADDRESS.   A favorite pomposity of academia now spread like a fungus. *Address* a letter. Don't address a problem. Instead, deal with it, take it up, consider it, tackle it, cope with it.

ALTERNATELY/ALTERNATIVELY.   Don't confuse the two. The first means "by turns": *They traveled alternately by snowmobile and dog sled.* If only one were available, they would go by dog sled, or, *alternatively,* by snowmobile.

AMBIVALENT.   This word is sometimes misused for *ambiguous. Ambivalent,* a term from psychoanalysis, means that two irreconcilable emotions are operating in the mind (love-hate, for example). *Mixed feelings* is a less pretentious substitute. *Ambiguous* is applied only to written or spoken statements and means "having several possible meanings." *The employer was ambivalent about the applicant because of his ambiguous answers.*

ANTIQUE. The trouble with *antique* is that it is both a noun and an adjective. An antique is a rare old object. An antique clock is a rare old clock. If you want to describe a rare old store you could conceivably call it an antique store. But if you mean a store that trades in rare old objects, it is an antiques store. A person who deals in antique objects is an antiques dealer.

ANYMORE. When the *Webster III* dictionary came out, language purists were shocked that it permitted *any more* to be written as one word, *anymore*. Well, all right (NEVER *alright*), I don't like it a lot (NEVER *alot*), but will go along — with this reservation: When you're writing about something additional, make it two words: *I don't want any more advice from you.* When it's used as an adverb, as in, *I don't want to argue with that editor anymore,* go ahead and make it one word. By the way, if you've ever written *some place* as one word, don't do it any more.

CHARISMA. Properly a theological term for the special grace that gives saints their power; a divine gift. For lesser mortals, *appeal, magnetism, attractiveness,* all are more appropriate. Nowadays, *charisma* is used for any ward politican with a smooth voice and a knack for getting votes.

COMMUNITY. For some reason, perhaps because the bonds that make up a true community are scarce and getting scarcer, the noun is applied these days to professions, occupations and virtually any conglomeration of people sharing peripheral interests. So we see *medical community, engineering community, business community* and may soon see *trash collectors' community.* Write *doctors, engineers, business (people)* and, by all means, *trash collectors.*

CONCEPT. Pompous noun for *idea, notion, scheme.* Use one of those less grand words unless you're referring to something complex, like Einstein's concept of the universe, or Küng's concept of the church. Not *the mayor's new concept of parking lot use.* (Be careful of *notion,* though. It's often used as a sneer word, meaning a sort of harebrained idea: *He had a notion he could halt the arms race.*)

CONCEPTUALIZE.   Same thing. Fit for, say, an effort to conceptualize the movement of subatomic particles. But why bother? What's wrong with *envision*?

CONFRONTATION.   An all-purpose word from the seething Sixties that has long since turned mushy. When possible, reach for the specifics: *Noisy argument, shoving match, scuffle, exchange of insults, ultimatum.*

CONVINCE, PERSUADE.   *Convince* requires a state of mind, *persuade* a course of action. A person often acts in accordance with convictions, but not necessarily. The editor may try to convince you that a lead is poor; failing, he may persuade you to change it anyway. The distinction is valuable and should be preserved. Think: convince *that*, persuade *to.*

DICHOTOMY.   It means "a split or division into two contradictory or mutually exclusive parts": truth and falsehood, right and wrong. *Split* or *division* are always preferable in newswriting.

DILEMMA.   If we restrict this word (or any word) to its precise meaning we keep its usefulness. *Dilemma* is not a synonym of *predicament* or *jam* or *trouble.* It means that someone faces two alternative courses of action, both of which are likely to be unpleasant. "On the horns of a dilemma" is a cliché to be avoided, but it does illustrate the special problem the word defines.

DISINTERESTED.   Does not mean *un*interested. *Disin*-terested means personally detached, unbiased in a matter in which you have no stake. *Un*interested simply means lacking interest. You can be *dis*interested in your friend's divorce without being at all *un*interested. As a reporter you should always be *dis*interested but never *un*interested.

EXCELLENCE, PURSUIT OF.   Shopworn to the point anything associated with excellence should never be. A favored, if immodest, characterization by certain professional groups of their current scrambling. Sometimes unavoidable in direct quotes; use with extreme caution at other times.

EXPECT/ANTICIPATE.   Politicians and others given to pretentiousness often substitute *anticipate* for *expect*. The words do not mean the same and the distinction should be kept. To *expect* is simply "to look ahead to." *Citrus growers expect about the same production as last year.* The word *anticipate* means "to look ahead to — and do something about it." *They put smudge pots in the groves, anticipating frost.*

EXPLICATE.   If you like *replicate,* you'll love *explicate,* a pompous word for *explain.* Literary critics embrace it to sound important: *Nowhere is Mr. Thomas's exegesis more clearly explicated . . .* Extricate me!

FARTHER/FURTHER.   Correct usage requires *farther* when speaking of literal distance; *further* in all other instances. *My desk is farther from the water cooler than yours. Your daughter is further along in school than mine."* But be careful. The expression *taking it a step further,* for example, is correct because *step* is used metaphorically, not as a literal measure of distance.

FEWER/LESS.   That beer does not have less calories,

that beer has fewer calories. *Less* applies to quantities, *fewer* to numbers. Ironclad rule: *less* modifies a singular noun, *fewer* modifies a plural noun. Fewer calories, less taste.

FLAUNT/FLOUT. A TV announcer reported, "Doctors with MD plates sometimes flaunt the law." *Flaunt* means "boastfully exhibiting." If you've got it, flaunt it. *Flout* means "defy." What the doctors did with the MD plates was flout the law and flaunt their profession.

FORTUNATE/FORTUITOUS. Although some, seeking pomposity, substitute *fortuitous* for *fortunate,* the words are not synonymous. *Fortunate* means "lucky." *Fortuitous* means "by chance," "by accident." Something which is *fortuitous* can also be *fortunate,* but unless it happened by chance, *fortunate* is the correct word: *It was fortunate that the plane had enough fuel to reach an alternate landing field. The pilot's choice was fortuitous; all the other fields were damaged.*

FOUNDER/FLOUNDER. *Without steam, the pumps could not function and the ship began to flounder and go down.* No, it didn't. It began to *founder,* that is "to collapse, to break down suddenly." To *flounder* means "to move clumsily, awkwardly, in confusion" — probably a blend of *founder* and *blunder.* (When that foundering ship sank, a flounder [noun] might have watched.)

FROM . . . TO. This construction denotes a logical progression, as from A to Z or from girlhood to womanhood, or from stock room to board room, or from soup to nuts. To write *activities that range from golf to investing* begs the question; what goes between? To write *from golf to investing to racing to poker* is worse. What you probably mean is *as diverse as.* If so, say so.

FUELED. Badly overused. Moreover, *fueled* to mean "fed" or "increased" is not often heard in conversation, a fact that should always arouse suspicion. We don't say, *My sister-in-law's sudden arrival further fueled my annoyance.* The word is simply burned out. Try another.

FULSOME. It does not mean "lavish" or "bountiful," as in *fulsome praise*. It means "revolting, noisome." The word is now so often misused that a lot of people will misunderstand when you use it correctly. The literate, who are also part of the readership, will applaud. This does, however, raise the point of *fulsome*'s usefulness. There are plenty of substitutes.

GUARDED CONDITION. An illiteracy that's making headway because it seems to mean something. A patient's condition, however, is not guarded. The prognosis is. The doctor is *guarded* in forecasting the outcome. If a cop is posted in the hospital room, then a patient is in guarded condition.

HOPEFUL/FEARFUL/THANKFUL. They were thankful that he had returned, fearful that he might be ill, and hopeful that he would recover. A $10,000 reward for proof that these words improve upon, *They were grateful that he had returned, feared he might be ill, and hoped he would recover.* (The battle against *hopefully*, used in the sense of "we hope" [*Hopefully the Dodgers will win the pennant.*] seems hopeless — hopefulless? — but fight on.) These formulations have already betrayed at least one writer into *she said shamefully*, when she meant *shamefacedly*. For shame.

IMPACT. Much overused. As a noun, *effect* is almost always better. As a verb, *impact* is vintage bureaucratese; use *affect*.

INFER/IMPLY.   *The official complained that the news-paper story falsely <u>inferred</u> that he had condoned racial hatred.* The word the writer intended was *implied. Infer* means "to deduce or judge from evidence." *Imply* means "to intimate, to signify, to hint."

INNOVATIVE.   Ridden hard by advertising copywriters and institutional and political boasters and propagandists, this adjective is nearly exhausted. Few programs, policies or people are truly original. Reserve the word for such rare instances. Renaming three courses in its curriculum doesn't make Podunk College an *innovative* school.

INPUT.   Nice computer term, so let's keep it in the technical kennel. In human affairs, warm-blooded words are better: *They sought a stronger voice, or a greater say, at city hall,* not *more input.*

INTERFACE.   A technical word from science and engineering that jargoneers find irresistible. It means a connection between independent systems, as between a computer and a typesetting machine. Showoffs apply it to human relations, where *coordination, agreement, something in common, shared,* all are better terms. *Doctors and nurses should interface more in a hospital setting* might be tough if many wear glasses. Why not work together? Do we interface on this point?

KUDOS.   The Greeks had a word for it and it was kydos, meaning "glory." It has come to us almost intact as *kudos,* meaning "acclaim in recognition of achievement." It is a good word to avoid because it often sounds wrong when used correctly, as *kudos is in order for Joe Smith.* Although some dictionaries, yielding to its misuse, regard *kudos* as both singular and plural, it is, strictly speaking, a singular noun in the same way that *pathos,* of similar Greek origin, is singular. There is no such word as *kudo* just as there is no such word as *patho*. If you simply avoid *kudos* it will be to your glory.

LEGENDARY.   Crops up now and then in the hype mode: *Johnny Bench, the legendary catcher*. He's nothing of the sort. A legend is a story handed down from earlier times that's widely believed to be true; the legend of the headless horseman, for example. It's still a myth, though, which Johnny Bench isn't. The epithet was applied by a headless writer.

LIFESTYLE.   Overworked vogue word, usually just a flossy way of saying *life* or *way of living*. *After years of comfort and luxury, financial setbacks changed his lifestyle (life). Some Acapulcans have a splendid lifestyle (live splendidly)*. It is time for this trendy locution to die, in style.

LITERALLY.   Disastrous as a casual intensifier because it means that something is factually and precisely true. *The Mets literally slaughtered the Cardinals last night* would have left at least nine corpses. I would never use *literally* in a million years. I mean that figuratively.

MEDIA.   This word is plural. The press is a news *medium*, television is a *medium*, radio is a *medium*. Together they are news *media*. Never write, *The media is sometimes guilty of bad grammar*. Write, *The media are*. . .

MILITATE/MITIGATE.   The words are confusing because they sound and look alike. They aren't the least similar in meaning. *Militate* (from the Latin word for soldier) means "to have weight or effect." *Mitigate* (from the Latin "to soften") means just that: "to soften, make less severe or painful, alleviate, mollify." *The judge mitigated the sen-*

tence from 30 days to 10. The unpredictable economy militates against long-term planning. Choose plainer words.

NAVAL. This maritime adjective sometimes comes out *navel,* always good for a belly laugh. The variety of orange, though, is correctly *navel,* because that's what that scar resembles where it was attached, umbilically, to a blossom.

NOTION. See CONCEPT.

NOUNS INTO VERBS. Turning nouns into verbs has a long and honorable tradition: *to telephone, to cable,* and the more recent *to bus. To contact* is borderline usage, handy only when the nature of the contact is nebulous: letter, telephone call, native runner? But draw the line at noun-spawned verbs that serve no real need and sound gushy, like *debut, host, author.* People make their debuts, give parties, write books. Especially execrable is *debut* in the past tense: *The new edition debuted three months ago.*

OBJECTIVE. No one important likes to have a mere aim or goal, but an objective. In most uses, *aim* or *goal* is better.

ONLY. Be careful when you place this trouble-fraught little modifier. Put *only* before any word in the following seven-word sentence and you get seven different meanings: *I hit him in the eye yesterday.* But don't get pedantic about it. In such commonly understood phrases as *I only want orange juice,* placement of *only* where it strictly belongs (before *orange juice*) seems stilted. I'm only trying to help.

OPTION. If you don't like this word, which bureaucrats and academic babblers have made *de rigueur,* you have an option: *choice.* Same with the verb *opt*: choose *choose.*

PERCEIVE.   Blown-up word for *see, understand, grasp, realize,* spewn into the conversational mainstream via academia. Through overuse for the sake of perceptual elegance, also becoming a weasel word, beclouding the obvious. *Jamaica's economic decline under Prime Minister Manley was perceived as a major cause of his defeat.* Perceived, because it was. Omit *perceived as.*

PLUS.   Advertisers kidnapped this innocent word from mathematicians as a trendy replacement for *also,* or *moreover* or *not only that, but,* none of which needs replacing. Let us restore *plus* to the mathematicians. Minus, never start a sentence with it.

PRAGMATIC.   Imported from philosophy, where it means the intellectual acceptance of whatever is workable as "true," or at least sound. A pragmatist may dislike phonics in principle, but accept it as a workable way to teach reading. But if somebody knows how to deal with insurance salesmen, bank statements and a leaky faucet, he's not pragmatic, he's practical.

PRE-DAWN DARKNESS.   Hackneyed journalese. Write *pre-dawn darkness* if you're also prepared to write *pre-dusk brightness.* It is a poetic phrase that has been worked to death, that's all. A substitute is needed. How about *ere Aurora arose?* No? Then let us return, simply, to *before dawn.*

PRESTIGIOUS.   This, along with *coveted,* is an automatic modifier that pops up drearily with award, trophy, honor. You even see *the prestigious Nobel Prize* and *the coveted Pulitzer Prize.* It goes without saying, so don't say it.

REASON WHY.   When *reason* is used as a noun, try

never to follow it with *why*. The reason I urge this (not the reason *why* I urge this) is to reduce clutter. *Why* after reason is almost always superfluous. When the tone is conversational, though, it's sometimes hard to avoid the *why* — but I see no reason why rules should not have exceptions, do you?

REFER.   Refer *back* is tautological; it's the only way to go. Same is true of revert *back*. That *re* prefix means back. Redundant.

REFUTE/REBUT.   A subtle distinction here, but important, especially in journalism, to avoid editorializing unwittingly. *Refute* renders a verdict; it means "to disprove, to demolish an argument." *Rebut* means "to answer charges or allegations by counter-argument." Even though most dictionaries give *rebut* the secondary meaning of "disprove," the word isn't safe. *Reply to, contend, contradict* are neutral substitutes for *rebut* and probably better than *refute.*

RELATE TO.   A vogue term, probably from the social sciences, with a dogged power of endurance. Its vagueness masks any interesting specifics of the relationship. If little Mary fails to relate to her peers, she may be a bully, she may be shy, or she may limp. For these or other reasons, she can't seem to make friends. That's a human way of putting it.

REPLICATE.   Scientists like to use *replicate* instead of *repeat exactly,* or *duplicate.* Let 'em.

RESUPPLY.   Military planners seem to favor this redundancy. If bringing more provisions to the embattled garrison is a resupply, do the troops then re-eat and re-shoot them? Just make it *supply.*

SCENARIO.   Tom Barber, word-watcher at the *Milwaukee Journal*, calls it "one of those tiresome Watergate words, coined by a bunch of generals, probably, as they plotted deploying their deterrent firepower to neutralize an aggressor." Amen. Barber made a list of 99 alternate words. He wasn't even breathing hard.

SELF-CONFESSED.   Until you discover a way for someone to confess in another person's behalf, write *confessed*.

SHAMBLES.   We read expressions like, *The nursery was a shambles*, intended to mean the kiddies had left toys scattered about. A shambles is a slaughterhouse (and is never used in the singular, which is a gait). When I read *shambles* in the sense of merely untidy or disheveled, I'm out for blood.

SKILLS.   Pedagogues' padding. *Mastering mathematical skills, teaching reading skills.* Make it *mastering mathematics, teaching to read.*

SOPHISTICATED.   A cliché adjective that writers apply to any piece of technology that's over their heads. Computers, as a class, for example, are no longer so remarkable that they need to be tagged as sophisticated. Neither are F-16s. Because so much is, in comparison with the ordinary writer's mechanical aptitude, sophisticated, the adjective should be used sparingly.

SPELLING.   The English language embraces so many variations in spelling that some words, like the multiplication tables, just have to be memorized. Start with these 20 and add your own: *accommodate, affidavit, asinine, consensus, diphtheria, embarrass, harass, imposter, impresario, inoculate, liquefy, pavilion, precede, rarefy, resuscitate, rococo, sacrilegious, siege, supersede, titillate.*

STANCE.   Means primarily a standing position, as a fighter or golfer might take. Now it is used for attitude, position, philosophy: *his foreign policy stance.* There's nothing drastically wrong with it except that it's becoming worn out, like posture.

STRATEGY.   Bow-wow language. Use *plan, scheme, design, method. The housing agency has several strategies for dealing with urban poverty* sounds important in a handout, which is why it's there. Make it *has several ways of dealing with poverty.* Academics, of course, will talk about *new strategies in curricular reform,* but there is no redeeming them.

SUBSUME.   As soon as academics began sprinkling their learned papers with this vogue word, bureaucrats jumped all over it. Most of them misuse it. *Subsume* means "to include within a larger group." *The question of twice-weekly garbage pickup was subsumed by the debate over the whole municipal budget.* Probably because it looks and sounds like *consume,* some mistakenly take it to mean "to eat up." Don't you.

SUPPORTIVE OF.   Why weaken a decent verb by turning it into an adjective with a preposition? *He was supportive of the fund drive*? What mush. *He supported the fund drive.*

SURROGATE.   Hard to know, or judge, how this word invaded political babble, as in *the President's surrogates. Representatives, stand-ins, substitutes* are better words, although politicians will prefer the more imposing one.

TENSIONS, RELAXATION OF.   Staple of diplomatic language, where vagueness is often useful. Overblown when used for more mundane affairs, such as a school board squabbling with teachers, a baseball manager at odds with the owner. (Is it a *détente* if they become friendly again?) *The fact that contract negotiations with the meat packers resumed signaled a relaxation of tensions.* Make it *brightened hopes for a settlement,* or some such.

THRUST.   Doesn't blast off quite as frequently as it used to, but it's still tired and, by association with the types who keep using it as a noun, pompous. *The thrust of the 21-page report*. . . Make it *gist, tenor, drift, burden.*

UTILIZE.   No discernible reason why anyone would want to substitute that verb for *use.* They have exactly the same meaning, so why choose the longer and ugly word over the short and crisp one? Use *use.*

VERBAL/ORAL.   *Verbal* applies to any use of language, either spoken or written. *Oral* applies to spoken language only. *He made a <u>verbal</u> commitment* is nonsense.

VIABLE.   In its original sense in the life sciences, *viable* means "capable of survival and growth." Now it is used for *real, workable, practical, sound, healthy.* If those splendid words needed technical reinforcement, *viable* would be all right. But there is no need for it, and, besides, misuse robs *viable* of a limited and precise meaning.

VIABLE ALTERNATIVE.   Used in *viable's* (regrettably) expanded sense to mean "a sound or workable alternative." But does anyone ever seek an unsound or unworkable alternative? The adjective is redundant; leave it out. The same often applies to modifiers for *solution* and *option**.

---

*—*The* (Toronto) *Globe and Mail* quoted a doctor who carried the locution to the absurd: "If someone is confronted with certain knowledge that he or she is going to die a painful death through terminal illness, then suicide can be a viable option."

VIRTUAL. It doesn't mean "actual," and it doesn't mean "nearly," either. *Virtual* means that something has the effect but not the form. *When the president resigned, the vice president became the <u>virtual</u> head of the company* (even though he had not been so named).

WHENCE, ALBEIT, WHEREIN, THUS. All somewhat archaic and therefore (not hence) undesirable. But if you must use *whence,* it means "from where"; *from whence* is tautological.

WORKAHOLIC. This was a bright coinage back when it identified a person truly addicted to work. Now it has been reduced to describing anyone who stays late at the office. Time to put it aside to dry out — along with all the other *aholics*: *cleanaholic* (tidy housekeeper), *runaholic* (jogger), and, so help me, *wordaholic* (scrupulous editor). I need a drink.

YOUTH. A respectable noun which few ever use in conversation. You talk about children, adolescents, teen-agers, young people, the youth of America, perhaps, but can you hear yourself saying, *Suzie next door is an interesting youth*? No? Then think twice before you use the word in copy.